Hans Mol i...gi.... .. ....i.i. ....i.i.d in 1948 and was ordained into the Presbyterian ministry in 1952. After working among Dutch migrants in Australia, he pursued his academic interests in the USA, leading to a doctorate in sociology from Columbia University in 1960.

After a lectureship in New Zealand from 1961 to 1963 and a fellowship in Australia from 1963 to 1970, he became professor in the sociology of religion at McMaster University, Toronto, Canada, a position he still holds.

He has lectured widely and been very active in professional organisations. From 1963 to 1969 he was the secretary-treasurer of the Sociological Association of Australia and New Zealand. From 1970 to 1978 he was first secretary and subsequently president of the Sociology of Religion Research Committee of the International Sociological Association.

Hans Mol is married with four children.

How God Hoodwinked Hitler

HANS MOL

An Albatross Book

© Hans Mol 1987

Published in Australia and New Zealand by
Albatross Books Pty Ltd
PO Box 320, Sutherland
NSW 2232, Australia
and in the United Kingdom by
Lion Publishing
Icknield Way, Tring,
Herts HP23 4LE, England

First edition 1987

National Library of Australia
Cataloguing-in-Publication data

Mol, Hans, 1922
How God Hoodwinked Hitler

Simultaneously published: Tring, Herts:
Lion Publishing

ISBN 0 86760 037 3 (Albatross)
ISBN 0 7459 1197 8 (Lion)

1. Mol, Hans, 1922– — Imprisonment, 1943–1945.
2. World War, 1939–1945 — Prisoners and prisons, German —
Biography. 3. World War, 1939–1945 — Personal
narratives. 4. Christian biography. I. Title.

940.54'72'430924

Cover photo: John Waterhouse
Typeset by Rochester Communications Group, Sydney
Printed by Australian Print Group, Maryborough

Contents

Introduction

I WAS ONLY TWENTY-ONE WHEN THE GESTAPO
came and picked me up. It was the afternoon of the 22nd of
December, 1943. Two of my friends had already disappeared
in the morning and nobody knew where they were. Fearing
the worst, I had gone back to a room I shared with one of
them and destroyed whatever could be construed as evidence against us, such as letters and anti-Nazi leaflets.

My parents were farmers in the central region of the
Netherlands. Although they had been badly hit by the
Depression, they had sent me at considerable expense to the
Gymnasium, an elite category of Dutch high schools, and
from there to the University of Amsterdam where I had
begun courses in economics. But the war had begun to inter-
fere with those studies and in 1943 the German occupying
forces permitted only those students who signed an oath of
loyalty to continue their work. Nazism was an abomination
to almost all of us and so only a small percentage signed. The
rest either hid or were put to work in Germany. I was sent
to a little German factory town, Kleinwanzleben. Yet even in
the heart of the enemy's territory our zeal for democracy
remained unflagging. We worked with many French and
Russian prisoners of war and we kept their anti-Nazi spirits
high with the BBC news which we picked up on a clandestine
radio receiver. This was our undoing.

The Gestapo camp where we ended up was another world.
Our youthful exuberance had to cope with cruelty and inhu-

manity. Bashing of prisoners and freezing parades in thin clothing were the order of the day. Our anti-Nazi crusade for democracy and human rights became dampened by such mundane necessities as louse hunting and bowel movement when the stinking pot in the corner was already overflowing.

Up to December 1943, religion had been unimportant to me. My grandfathers on both sides had been elders of the Reformed Church, but my parents had become increasingly disillusioned with religion. To them it unduly constrained the forces of social reform, particularly in the area of rent legislation for farmers who were at the mercy of the rich owners. I was the only one of my family who went to church at all regularly, but only because I liked the little organ which I was allowed to play for services occasionally. The Barthian drivel from the pulpit was, I thought, irrelevant.

Yet in the Gestapo camp and later prison this unintelligible preaching, insofar as I remembered it, began gradually to make sense. My easy student view of the world — if only Nazism can be eradicated everything will be fine — began to be replaced slowly by a sense of the inevitability of evil not just in others, but also in myself. Wasn't this mixture of good and bad both in the SS guards and in my fellow prisoners called 'sin' in the drivel I had so decisively rejected in my youth?

And then there was all this enormous suffering around me. I began to detect broken spirits as much, if not more, amongst those who inflicted the physical suffering as amongst those who were its recipients. They stuck so pitifully to their much vaunted authority. Their puny souls were so precariously vexed by their vulnerable insecurity. There were moments when memories of the suffering Christ washed over me like a flood, miraculously converting all these horrible experiences into a deep glow of understanding. Was *that* God's promise of salvation? If it was, it was certainly big enough not just to help me cope but, far more importantly, to face death fearlessly.

I survived the Nazi holocaust. It changed me. I had gone

in as an innocent youth with some vague notions about the goodness of human reason and intentions. I came out of it as a chastened adult with a deep, ingrained sense of tragedy, overspread with the golden insights of a Christian faith. Not that the latter was now all that firm. Maturity and faith go together and who can ever claim to have arrived at either? But there was enough strength to withstand the despair and meaninglessness whenever they reared their ugly heads in later life.

What follows in this book is the story of Christian growth during the darkest period of my life. I began to write it quite by accident. In 1982, one of my colleagues in the Department of Religious Studies at McMaster University in Canada was teaching a course on death and dying. Hearing that I had been near death several times in Gestapo camps and German prisons during World War II and that death had come to mean little to me, he asked me to address his students. The class had been using the literature on the holocaust and some of the students had become interested in whether a God who allowed these atrocities could actually exist, an issue raised by a number of Jewish authors. In the lecture I took the opposite point of view and showed with examples how my own Christian faith had grown during the imprisonment and confrontation with death, and how without it religion might very well have remained irrelevant for me.

The class had been very responsive to the lecture and around the dinner table that night I told my wife and children about the discussion. They knew very little about my Gestapo camp exploits, partly because the Nazi world was completely alien to them, partly because I did not want them to have erroneous ideas about valour (if anything I had been an anti-hero), but mainly because the memories of these years were particularly painful. For decades I had found talking or writing about them unpleasant and uncomfortable.

That day it all changed. After almost forty years, my qualms had disappeared. And the more I talked, the more they insisted that it all be written down.

'Oh,' I said, 'it was done in April 1945 when I was recovering at my uncle's place in Ellewoutsdijk in Zeeland.'

I got out the old, yellowing manuscript, but it was in Dutch which they could not read. Worse, the content appalled me. Although factual, it was an arrogant piece of work and so disorganised. Embarrassing bits were left out and too many boring details were left in. The work needed to be completely re-written and interpreted.

I wrote a number of articles based on the early part of the manuscript for journals in Canada, Australia and New Zealand which were well received, one even receiving a best feature award at the annual Canadian Church Press banquet on 29 September, 1983.

But the format did not lend itself well to the coherent picture of Christian growth I had in mind and so I wrote the story as chapters of a book in chronological order.

The title of this book — *How God hoodwinked Hitler* — occurred to me halfway through the writing. It represented the humorous side of even the most lamentable events. But more seriously, it expressed the growing awareness that God steadily outstripped Nazism and other ideologies which put man's achievements and power at the centre of creation. The slow emptying of my old, threadbare identity and its unobtrusive yet inexorable filling with Christ seemed to me the crux of what I wanted to say. Hitler's rampaging, conquering might steamrolling over anguished souls and countries had disregarded God's still, small voice which worked away quietly. The impressive fury and foam of the Reich succumbed to the suffering Servant who gathered in his arms all the victims of Hitler's fuming. Only some of them have lived to tell the story and, as one of the survivors, I feel it incumbent upon me to do so.

This book also takes issue with the idea expressed in some of the holocaust literature that an omnipotent God could not possibly have allowed such savage barbarism. God therefore does not exist, so the argument goes, and we may as well recognise the world for what it is, godless. Over against this

I maintain that this view is too utopian in that it assumes that God's existence and God's order being established in all its glory are one and the same. I take the view that man's disorder, only slightly covered with cultural veneer, is an existential 'given', but that redeeming qualities are also provided. Sin and salvation, bestiality and Christian integrity existed side by side in camps and prisons and the more I matured, the clearer it became to me that the latter was the only effective antidote to the former, that it was actually vanquishing the other. This is the story of that discovery.

The book before you has improved greatly because of my wife's help with my English and the dedication of the word-processors in the Department of Sociology in the Institute of Advanced Studies of the Australian National University where I was offered a visiting fellowship during my 1983/84 sabbatical from McMaster University in Canada.

Hans Mol
Sydney, Australia
30 June, 1986

Part I
Gestapo Camp Rothensee

1

Interrogation

INTERROGATION BY THE GESTAPO proved to be a casual affair. No torturing. No deprivation of sleep. No all-night sessions. No strong lights aimed at my face. Just an avuncular officer with a beer belly asking questions from behind a desk in a cluttered office. Almost apologetically he produced a sizeable number of area maps he had confiscated from my room. What was I doing with them? Did I need them for helping the enemy to infiltrate? Fortunately he did not believe so himself and he seemed satisfied when I told the truth: I loved hiking, I had taken geography courses at the University of Amsterdam and I had bought them at the local bookstore.

Now, however, he became more serious. From somewhere on his untidy desk he fished out two freshly typed sheets of paper and began to read. The pieces proved to be the confessions of my two friends who had been detained earlier that day. They stated that we had listened to the enemy broadcasts of the British Broadcasting Corporation, prohibited by German law and, worse, that we had spread the English version of the news amongst French prisoners of war. This was a rather serious war crime to the Germans and could carry the death penalty. All foreigners were eyed with suspicion. They were compelled to keep the German war machine humming so that the natives could be spared for the front. To the Germans, we were a necessary evil: without us industry would be mortally crippled; but with us they held a potential source of sedition and moral corruption to their bosom and so they were overly sensitive to even innocuous gossip.

After the Gestapo officer finished reading, he handed me the sheets. They were indeed signed by my friends. I badly needed time and so I re-read the statements, furiously thinking of a way out. But I could not see any and so I signed a similar document. The avuncular spirit re-appeared as if by magic. The fat one looked at his watch and discovered, I imagine, that he had time after all to go for a beer at his favourite Bierstube. I was led to a cell, my interrogator still glowing with satisfaction from a difficult day's work done well.

In the cell my friends greeted me with bated breath.

'Did you know that we were picked up by the Gestapo on the street?'

'No, how did it happen?'

'Well, a policeman came by and asked us to go to the station. He would follow us from a distance. He politely requested our cooperation and suggested that we treat it all very casually, in order to raise as little fuss as possible.'

'What happened when you got there?'

'We were interrogated separately for what seemed hours. Then each of us had to sign statements covering the discussion.'

'Yes, I saw those. He made me read them before I was asked to sign my own.'

'Did you have a chance to destroy the incriminating anti-Nazi leaflets in our room before it was searched?'

'Yes I did.' They were overjoyed. They felt that a transgression of the broadcasting laws was minor compared with possession of printed anti-Nazi leaflets. And they were right!

'But how did you guess that there was trouble?'

'Well, both of you were unaccountably absent at lunchtime. I had an uneasy sense of foreboding. Something appeared to have gone seriously wrong. I did not know what, but the feeling was strong enough to make a special trip to our room and tear the leaflets into tiny little pieces. I threw them in the wastepaper basket. I was lucky that the bits were so small. During the search the officer actually inspected the wastepaper basket, but it would have taken hours to put the puzzle together and so he decided against it. Three cheers for Gestapo laziness!'

'Even this cloud seems to have a silver lining.'

'But why did you confess? What evidence did the Gestapo have?' I asked.

'You remember the letter we had been so worried about in September?'

I did. One of them had written an anti-Nazi letter to his family in the Netherlands. It was supposed to have been smuggled across the border, but was intercepted and all of us had worried about possible repercussions. However, it had happened more than ten weeks ago and so we had begun to relax.

'Well, a German translation of that letter was read to me,' said the oldest of our group who had been the first to be interrogated. 'I never read the original, but seeing that you (pointing to number two in our group) had been so worried, I assumed that the translation was accurate and so I confessed that indeed we had listened to the BBC and had spread its news amongst prisoners of war.'

'But,' interrupted the writer of the letter,' that is not what I wrote at all! I never mentioned the BBC. I expressed all sorts of anti-Nazi sentiments and hopes for a speedy defeat of Germany, but our clandestine radio was about the only thing that I did not mention!'

'Why then did you sign the confession?' I asked the writer.

'He never so much as talked about that letter. He just told me what you had said and confessed. I signed on the basis of your statement which he carefully and slowly read aloud and then allowed me to inspect,' said the writer.

'Then the translation must have been fake!'

We had walked into the Gestapo trap as lambs to the slaughter. It had shut behind us as securely as our cell door with its bolt and double lock. Our guilelessness had proved no match for Gestapo shrewdness. And understandably so. We did not belong to a well-oiled, carefully organised Dutch underground which presumably could match wits with the enemy. We shared with ninety-five per cent of the occupied, freedom-loving Dutch population a sentiment that was strongly anti-Nazi. And yet the Germans were as afraid of us as they were of the underground. To them the sapping of morale was as dangerous as — perhaps more so than — military sabotage.

Yet guilelessness proved to be our salvation. It was not until much later that we learnt that naievity had saved the life of each of us. Without confession we would have been transported to a concentration camp and certain death. Now we had committed an indictable offence for which there was proof. Now we could be handled by the German system of courts and prisons, where the survival rate was much higher. By guilelessly confessing, we unknowingly allowed the Gestapo to take us to court. The secret police instilled a holy fear in the population by mopping up what were often innocuous sources of anti-Nazism. But it immeasurably increased the 'holy fear' through covering its sources of information: nobody knew who could be trusted. To be effective, the Gestapo had to rely on faked evidence, producing confessions which could take the place of testimony by its own sources.

There had been nothing heroic or Christian about our guilelessness. Yet it had saved us. Later, I did meet Christians who much more awesomely lived the injunction of Jesus to go out like lambs amongst the wolves and much more effectively proved the power of simple Christian trust in the face of overwhelming odds. I remember a Jehovah's Witness on the third floor of the prison in Magdeburg in the spring of 1944. He was in his late thirties. Hitler had outlawed the Witnesses. They had fearlessly attacked the evil foundations of Nazism and continued to do so after being driven underground. The Witness on the third floor had been found guilty in court, but continued to rail at the godlessness of Nazism to anybody, high or low, prepared to listen.

When I met him he was as thin as a rake, but his eyes sparkled with conviction. Couldn't I see that the Book of Revelation spoke about the events happening before our very eyes? Hitler was the anti-Christ and the war was nothing if not the last ghoulish spasm of the forces of Satan, seemingly victorious, but doomed to destruction. Christ, the Lamb of God, was seated on the throne and nothing the Nazis could do — killing him for instance — would in any way alter the course of events. The Nazi wolves would be utterly destroyed and the helpless lambs would triumph. If the Nazis were to shorten his own miserable life, so much the better. The Saviour would recruit him in his heavenly army and he would be privileged beyond his wildest dreams.

I was reminded of him when a few years ago I read Solzhenitsyn's first volume of *The Gulag Archipelago*. The Russian author asked himself the question: 'What do you need to make you stronger than the interrogator and the whole trap?' And then he gave his own answer: 'You must say to yourself: my body is useless and alien to me. Only my conscience and my spirit remain precious.' Confronted with such a prisoner, the interrogation will tremble, Solzhenitsyn concluded, and gave the example of an old woman who had harboured the escaped Metropolitan of the Orthodox Church in Moscow. The interrogators went after her in groups, as they had to find out more about the underground railroad of believers. They shook their fists in the little old woman's face, but she said: 'There is nothing you can do with me, even if you cut me into pieces. After all, you are afraid of your bosses, and you are afraid of each other. You are even afraid of killing me... but I am not afraid of anything. I would be glad to be judged by God right this minute.'

The power of the powerless. The strength of the defenceless. The defiance of the non-resister. They don't fit into the Macchiavellian rules of political games, or the sophisticated manoeuvres of bureaucratic empires. And yet they exist. Even better, they make existence eminently more just and profound. It took me years to learn that lesson. Without the Gestapo camp and the German prisons I might have never learnt it. But, like Solzhenitsyn, it helped me to become a Christian. Christianity puts the Lamb upon the throne. It proclaims that there is more to life than the wolves of guile, intrigue and tyranny, however close we still are to our animal instincts. And it is not less realistic for insisting that the Saviour is not a wolf, but a Lamb.

2

Bashing

THE CELL IN THE KLEINWANZLEBEN Police Headquarters was a rather primitive sort of affair. It had a stove
and plenty of fuel, but there was no outlet for the smoke. Nor
was there a toilet and the next morning the policeman took
each of us separately to the one in the nearby town hall. At
about 10.00 a.m. he decided it was time to move us from
Kleinwanzleben. We climbed in the back of his little sedan
with room for two only. However, he was not about to make
two trips, so we had to fit as well as we could. The roads were
icy and progress was slow.

I remember how amicable and decent the policeman was
during the journey. In retrospect, I am sure that he wanted
to be kind to people about to end their earthly career. After
my release, the Lutheran minister of Kleinwanzleben
reported the policeman saying that we were destined for the
concentration camp. Therefore everyone assumed that our
arrest was not only the end of our freedom, but also of life.
No-one ever returned from concentration camps and therefore our belongings became fair game for anyone needing
books, clothing and anything else of value.

The car came to a halt near a muddy path north of Magdeburg. We staggered out, pleased to be able to stretch our
legs. We walked some distance to what proved to be the gate
of the Rothensee Gestapo camp. Here the policeman left us
in the hands of a fierce looking SS man who took a good look
at us and decided that above all else we needed a crash

course in standing at attention. He did not look as though he would stand foolishness and so we proved to be quick learners. Satisfied with the effect, he took us inside where all our belongings were confiscated.

The camp consisted of a drab collection of barracks surrounded by a double barbed wire fence. In its short existence it had already developed its own set of perverse traditions. On arrival, a newcomer was forthwith coerced into 'fall and crawl' exercises on the sharp gravel at the centre of the camp. An SS guard barked the commands and, if a prisoner was too slow, the fierce campdog was let loose. Either way a victim would be unrecognisable after the exercise. If the sharp gravel had not made a mess of his bare parts and clothing, the dog would finish the roughhousing. For some unfathomable reason — it probably had something to do with personnel being short or on Christmas leave — we were spared the traditional introduction to camp life. However, that same day we were put to strengthening and repairing the inner barbed wire fence and our dishevelment soon matched that of the others.

I was assigned to barrack 7, a badly built, drafty, louse-infected hut of five metres by eight metres with thirty bunkbeds arranged around a woodstove which either burnt too well or not at all. My fellow inmates came from all over Europe. There were some other Dutchmen, half-a-dozen French and Belgians, a few Russians, Poles, Czechs and Serbs, one Spaniard, one Italian, one Croat and a German who was in charge and the apparent ear of the Gestapo. There was a hierarchy according to the day of one's admission: those who had arrived most recently got the draftiest bunkbed without a straw mattress. If one had been there a while, one might inherit a better spot and at least something between oneself and the bare boards. Yet a mattress was a mixed blessing. While sleeping on planks only, my attraction for lice was minimal, but as soon as I became 'luckier', the lice had a field day!

The camp served a number of purposes. It was first of all

a sorting station for detainees: those who could be handled by the German system of courts and prisons, and those who opposed Nazism and were usually consigned to concentration camps. It was also designed to strike terror in the hearts of those perverts who through word or action made fun of the sacred destiny of the German Reich. Or worse still, those artless individuals who were not above cracking jokes about the greatest idol of all, the Fuhrer.

The sobering, detoxifying intentions of Rothensee became clear on the second day of our arrival. Just before lock-up time four young Frenchmen (they were barely out of high school) were pushed into our barrack. They were in considerable pain and could hardly walk, let alone sit. Their hair was shaved and their faces swollen with large bruises where they had been beaten. Three of them had black eyes and from what they told us their backs and bottoms were in even worse shape. A circle of countrymen and other foreigners soon formed around them. What had happened? They had been on the receiving end of the special treatment which the Gestapo reserved for those whom it considered excessively base and obnoxious.

What had they done? Well, the previous night they had had a party. They had drunk a couple of beers, after which one of them had carefully removed a large picture of Hitler from the wall. They had spread it on the floor, had formed a circle around it and relieved themselves on it in unison. While in the act some German party members had walked in. They lost no time calling the Gestapo and the 'treatment' had been meted out at Gestapo headquarters during the night.

No one in the camp was ever sure whether he was there to be 'detoxified' of anti-Nazi inebriation and then released or whether he was destined for prison and concentration camp. Nor did anyone know how long he would have to stay. Not being able to even guess what to expect had its own sobering and depressing effect. The Gestapo made full use of the manufactured climate of uncertainty. It calculated that cutting people loose from their moorings and leaving them in a suspended state of anxiety would make them more amenable. And most prisoners fell in line. They wanted their freedom almost at any price. At a minimum they wanted to know what to expect, and if outward conformity to Nazi norms was the means for getting out, they would gladly conform. Anything was better than confinement and ambiguity.

After a few days the French teenagers began to toe the line. And so did we. We kept a rein on any anti-Nazi sentiments, especially when there were Germans around. Instead, we talked a fair bit with other prisoners. Why were they here? What did they expect to happen? Did they know of others who had been released for similar crimes? How seriously was anti-Nazism punished? There was no clear pattern. There were rumours about the horrors of concentration camps, but then some others had apparently been set free after a bout at Rothensee. Most agreed that it was better to be an ordinary thief than to be a political suspect.

Yet the Gestapo could not prevent us from finding alternative sources of security, making our plight tolerable. The French teenagers created a more tightly knit bond of friendship. It was as though their common suffering had made them more careful with others and more intimate with one another. They formed a shell around themselves which only those who spoke French could penetrate. Language was the protective shield. My high school French was rather stilted, but I was only a few years older and also 'political'. And so they tried to speak somewhat less rapidly when I joined them. They were now very polite and well behaved with both German prisoners and guards, but their inward resentment really showed when they were amongst themselves. They could devastatingly mimic their captors. Their disdain for German bombast and pomposity was boundless, but they only indulged in the luxury of mimicry when no one else was around.

Friendship, however, was not the only antidote against Gestapo camp anxiety. Some people turned inward and withdrew, as though private peace was their first priority. One man in particular rarely mixed with the rest. He had his bunk in the back, farthest away from the entrance and at the opposite end from the stove which formed the social centre of the barrack. He was in his middle thirties and, like most of us, had been forced to work in German industry. He hailed from Budweis in Czechoslovakia where he had worked in an office. When he walked, he shuffled like a pensive philosopher. I never got out of him why he was in Rothensee. He was often reading a well-thumbed New Testament in Czech and, as it was the Christmas season, he had begun to re-read, he said, the beginning of the Gospel of John.

It was his favourite Gospel. The cosmic intentions of Christ's birth were best expressed, he thought, by St John. He had progressed to the third chapter which began with the story of Nicodemus, the Pharisee, who had come to Jesus at night. Nicodemus is obviously in turmoil and in conflict with himself and so Jesus says: 'You have to be born again', as though inner security could be procured from a drastic re-alignment of priorities. And the way to do this, the chapter implies, is to prefer spirit to flesh, heaven to earth and, above all, Christ to Satan. My fellow inmate then hesitatingly confessed that he had more in common with Nicodemus than the disciples, the unconverted than the converted. Yet he said: 'There is a certain comfort in reading the scriptures. It takes me back to the safe past. There was something then which was secure, whereas now even physical survival is in doubt. One does not know what to expect. Caprice seems to reign supreme.'

'Yet,' he continued sadly, 'if I were born again, even the past would not matter so much. I would have no worry about the future. The exalted present, the intoxication with Christ, would be more than enough to carry me through. But', he added somewhat quizzically, 'my very need to make sense of it all seems to make the Christ with whom Nicodemus spoke secondary. How can I be re-born when my identity is so precious that I cannot let go?'

He continued in this vein for some time. He obviously did not expect an answer from someone who had not even begun to think through the same issues. And yet I felt honoured that I, young though I was, had been taken into his confidence. It had probably come about because I was the only one in the barrack who had taken any notice of him. And he found it a relief to put at least some of his thoughts into words.

Whether it was through the safety of friendship or the memory of the Christian tradition, the inmates of the Rothensee Gestapo camp attempted to reconstruct a world which the secret police was bent on destroying. The outline of an ascertainable future was blurred in order that the Nazi ideology could fill the vacuum or would meet with minimum resistance. The Gestapo succeeded in blunting resistance, but it never converted anyone as far as I could discover. If anything, it stiffened the inner resolve of those whom it detained. I learnt from the clerk-philosopher of Budweis that there was an unobtrusive depth to the Nicodemus story which was relevant to our common predicament and that the compassionate Christ heals broken spirits even when they seem to be wholly at the mercy of an all-powerful enemy.

3

Christmas

ON CHRISTMAS EVE 1943 I was assigned to the post office crew. SS guards with rifles stood by while we were counted. Then they marched us to trucks parked some distance from the camp. The Magdeburg post office had been unable to handle the flood of parcels for soldiers, prisoners of war and foreign workers. The packages had all been stored in a large, unused shed of the abattoir and it was our job to sort them and carry them to the appropriate sections of the floor reserved for major German cities.

It was good to be inside and to be protected from the icy wind. Other crews were not so fortunate. The railway gang had to carry and fit rails while standing in ankle-deep water and mud. The previous day I myself had worked on a similarly odious workforce. It had been our job to load and unload gravel for the air-raid shelter of the camp. The wind had whistled around us, but my thick wintercoat had been up to it. It was on the way back from the pit that the trouble had started. We were ordered to lie on top of the gravel in the back of the truck, but there was little to hold on to. The truck driver had driven much too fast and we had been flung from one side to the other. Lying on our stomachs, we needed both hands to keep a firm grip on a rope strung across. Even so at one corner we were almost thrown off. The wind froze our hands and ears. The buttons on our coats could not stand the strain any longer and flew off. The dirt from the wet gravel ground itself into our faces and our clothes. When the truck came to a halt we had been more dead than alive and yet we had to get through more of these trips. Somehow I made it through the day, but at night I discovered that there were no buttons, needles or thread with which to mend the coat.

The post office work was heaven by comparison. My co-workers were almost all German political prisoners, mainly communists and social democrats. They had pulled a few strings to be on this particular gang. The heavier dirtier jobs went to foreigners whose German was too poor for string-pulling. I had no trouble with German language or German geography (it was necessary to know where the major cities were), but I suspect that I was put on the crew for the Gestapo to gauge the extent of my anti-Nazism.

How would I behave in this group of prisoners who to a man detested anything even faintly smelling of Nazism? Would I join in the fun? It was clear by now that every barrack and prison crew had its spies and that very little escaped the commandant's ear. Later in prison I learnt how the system operated from an inmate who had worked in the Rothensee office and had witnessed the 'gossip' of the Gestapo stoolpigeons while they were entertained by the SS. Most of the prisoners on the post office crew were beyond caring, however, and I had a sneaking admiration for them.

Actually, I found it very difficult *not* to come out in the open. During the morning break at 9.00 a.m. it had become the habit of this group to exchange the latest anti-Hitler jokes. It was done quite openly when the SS guards were out of earshot. I had my own storehouse of political humour. Yet I held back, although it was impossible not to smile on occasion. The experience of the last two days was too fresh in my mind. The Gestapo had proved to be everywhere and more than likely amongst the wags themselves. I had already begun to implement what later became an iron rule: never express anti-Nazi sentiments in German; do it exclusively in French and English and, even then, only with political prisoners you can trust.

Yet there were moments when I wondered whether maybe

I had become overly prudent. I particularly got to know one of the social democrats rather well and I was convinced that I could trust him. He had lived in a town not far from Klein-wanzleben and knew many people there. He knew about the system of informers, but courageously turned a deaf ear to all caution. He was a very independent spirit indeed! After my release I enquired about his whereabouts and learned that he had died of 'pneumonia' in a concentration camp. The Nazi who told me this added: 'It was entirely his own fault. If he had kept a bit more quiet, he would have been alive today.' Still, these non-conformists were essential for the revival of democracy and human rights in which I so strongly believed.

We shared the sorting shed with a group of Italian prisoners of war. They formed an interesting mixture of cheerful, quick-witted, but also nimble-footed individuals. A couple of them had become experts in locating tobacco in a Red Cross parcel. They knew exactly on what side and in what corner the package had to be damaged for the tobacco to pour out. It was then carefully caught in cupped hands and used as coinage for goods and services in their camp. Some of it also trickled into the exchange system of Rothensee Gestapo camp.

Certainly Christmas Eve proved to be less of a personal shock than the previous two days had been. And I returned to the camp that night somewhat more optimistic about my prospects. I might now resemble a tramp in my buttonless dirty coat, but the jokes had been good and the shed had protected us against the freezing wind. Yet back in the barracks I still had not managed to get a bunkbed with a mattress. I was cold and miserable in my drafty corner after the lights had been turned out.

In the bunkbed above me was a young Polish officer. He could not sleep either on Christmas Eve. Actually he seemed quite upset. In Dutch culture it was unheard of for any man, let alone an army officer, to cry. He stifled his obvious distress, but I was too close not to notice. I asked him quietly whether there was something I could do. He whispered back that this was the eighth Christmas Eve he could not be home on the farm near Posen and that it was all just too much. That was the end of the conversation because we did not want to awaken the other prisoners, but the episode is engraved on my mind. It was the beginning of a series of intimations of deep tragedy and suffering in people which always struck a very sensitive chord. In my rather sheltered life I had never experienced suffering of this kind before, especially among the young.

On Christmas Day we were locked in the barracks all day. It had begun to snow and, through the barred window, the camp ground and the industrial area beyond looked desolate. Inside there was much chatting and socializing. There was also some trading: usually tobacco for anything edible. Most prisoners managed to keep tiny stores of often stolen wares in the recesses of their mattresses, but I did not smoke, nor was I hungry at the time. Most conversations were in the *lingua franca*, German, but the group of young Frenchmen staged a few hilarious skits in their own language and I began to notice that political conversations — almost all anti-Nazi — were carried out in anything but German for fear that the Gestapo would be informed.

The midday meal consisted of a bowl of hot water with a few pieces of half-raw turnip. I gave my portion to the Polish officer in the bunk above. He had been arrested long before me and was ravenous. Christmas Day 1943 was the last day before liberation that I could afford to be choosy about food. Soon I would be as ravenous as he was. We struck up a conversation. He had been in the underground, been caught in the act and was fairly sure that it soon would end in execution. Actually he was preparing himself for a dignified exit and soon our conversation turned to religion.

Christmas Eve, in his large, close-knit family, was the most important day of the year, he explained. It was then that the *Oplatek* wafer, or holy bread, was broken after family squabbles and conflicts had been aired and reconciled. After this

Wigilia, or Christmas Eve supper, and the midnight mass would take place. The night before, he said, he had felt intolerably homesick. He knew that they all had been praying for him around the big table at the homestead and that, without him, they all felt the circle to be incomplete. And yet they were also proud of him. To be a good Catholic meant to be a good Pole and his subversive activities, he felt, were the duty of a good Catholic and Pole. This was also his family's view of things.

Then our conversation turned to the midnight mass. It was the atmosphere, he said, with all the candles, the procession up the aisle and the people which had given him the lift. But more strongly there was also a sense of the presence of the Virgin Mary and Christ which he remembered from the past. That, too, had come back to him the previous night. Sitting there with him on my lower bunkbed, it occurred to me that what I had imagined to be lonely despair wasn't that after all. It was something less sad. It was indeed a sense of being lost without one's family, community and church. It was also a sense of exhilarating support from afar for his Nazi defiance and its consequences. But in addition, mixed in his muffled cries had been a recognition and memory of mystical union with God in his predicament.

Being Dutch and Reformed I had some trouble at first to fully comprehend this mixture of melancholy, homesickness and religious fervour. But later it dawned on me that he was manfully and realistically preparing himself for his execution. To die as a good Pole and a good Catholic was, I began to realise, more important than to desperately wrap oneself in childhood memories and to deny the present. Strangely enough a heroic death for his country was not his sole source of strength, either. What seemed to console him was the idea that he had done the best he could and that his faith would carry him through to the bitter end.

I don't know what happened to him. I have even forgotten his name. We were like ships that pass in the night. The camp was primarily a reception camp for recently apprehended subversives and criminals and there was a constant coming and going of inmates. His story seemed to fit much better with the passion rather than the birth of Christ. And yet it was also peculiarly appropriate for Christmas in that the cruel darkness of the Nazi world had been penetrated by a light which had begun to shine in Bethlehem and which had broken the cocoon of death as it had begun to spin itself so menacingly around this young Polish officer. However hard it was, death could not claim him any more. The darkness of Nazism obviously could neither comprehend nor contain this light. It had been unobtrusively and miraculously transformed in a casual conversation on a bunkbed in a Gestapo camp.

4

Lice

THE CAMP WAS INFESTED with a relentless all-conquering army of lice. They seemed to hide themselves during day in the dark recesses of our mattresses or in the inaccessible seams of one's clothing. But at night the pitiless hordes would march forth over one's body and feast on its juices or whatever else they found so delectable on our starving carcasses. They were everywhere. They were so small and colourless and there were so many that squashing them seemed an impossible, unending task.

I should have known better, yet I complained to the trusty whom the Gestapo had put in charge of our barracks. Others, less innocent and more familiar with the secret police, kept mum. There were faint smiles on the faces of the more knowing fellow prisoners standing around when I voiced my exasperation, but I attributed this to the golden rule for inmate behaviour: 'Don't rock the boat or you will get hurt.' The trusty asked a few questions and then took off for the command post at the gate.

Now lice were regarded as a serious matter by the commandant. Once a complaint of this nature was lodged, the secret police were unstoppable. They could in no way be deterred from solving the problem in ruthless, double-quick fashion. They seemed to relish the peremptory process, even when the goal was absurd. Military precision, irrevocable action and robot-like execution of task appeared to have its own intrinsic rewards.

I suspect that it was this mindset which made the Gestapo so brutal and efficient. Their abhorrence of the whimsical was total. Like many SS men I encountered later, they had been through the agonizing economic and political insipidness of the Weimar Republic. Hitler had rescued them from indeterminacy and chaos and they had responded with a vengeance. Never again would they tolerate disorderliness! Subservience and rule became deity. Anything as messy as Christian love and understanding was banished resolutely from the mind. They had become as marionettes in a puppet play. The Christian understanding of man as infinitely valuable in the sight of God was to them romantic drivel.

And so the alarm was raised. I had set an unstoppable train in motion. Lice could exist and multiply a thousandfold for all they cared as long as they remained unmentioned. But as soon as they became official an entire program of eradication had to be devised as the rulebook demanded. The trusty became the centre of agitation at the command post, although the staff liked to take things easy on a Sunday afternoon. The lice issue was discussed at great length. Then the commandant had a brilliant thought.

'Is Mol the only one with lice or do others have them too?' he asked.

'He is the only one who has complained,' the trusty said.

'Go and find out whether there are any others,' was the reply.

Meanwhile back in Barrack 7 some of the other prisoners brought me up-to-date. Did I know about the Russian a few weeks ago who had said something about lice to the higher-ups?

I professed ignorance.

Well, he had been promptly deloused in a rather gruesome manner. First, they had him strip completely in an unheated room — it was January 1944 — and, while he shivered uncontrollably in sub-zero temperature, his clothes had been disinfected and washed. Then his gear had been handed back dripping wet with profuse apologies: there were no drying facilities! This had not been the end of his misery. The officer in charge had insisted that no single louse could possibly be found alive on his leaving. And so he had personally supervised a thorough scrubbing from head to toe under an ice-cold shower.

By the time the trusty arrived back in barrack 7 I had visions of all thirty inmates shivering uncontrollably in the nude while their clothes were being washed and me being held responsible for the ordeal. However, he had dealt with emergencies before. He called us all together.

'Is there anyone else with lice?' he boomed.

No answer.

'I have to know straightaway. The commandant is waiting,' he added. For those who had not heard the tale of the Russian, he then explained in detail what delousing meant and, by the time he had finished, no one had lice. Some prisoners were gratifyingly adamant and indignant. And so the trusty went back to the commandant with the report that even the question about lice had roused great indignation. This seemed to take a load off the commandant's mind and absolved him from further logistics.

'Anyone here not busy?' he enquired of his staff. They all had excuses.

'All right then,' he said, turning to the trusty, 'you delouse Mol.'

Back in Barrack 7 we were all waiting anxiously. Would the whole place with all its contents, mattresses and clothes have to be deloused? The trusty was a burly fellow from the underworld. He did not like his stoolpigeon job. He was constantly surrounded with suspicion and longed for affection. Now he had averted a calamity for the entire barracks.

The inmates were appropriately grateful and they all congratulated him on a job well done. For once the suspicions were lifted and he glowed in the aftermath. In addition, he had a soft spot in his heart for 'innocents' and 'idiots from the university', such as me. They were a welcome diversion from the crowd of toughs he always had to deal with. And so he decided not to be too hard on me who had started it all.

By this time it was dark. The trusty took me to the commandant who kept his distance from the source of infestation (me). He received the key for the barracks where the delousing was to take place. He opened the place but locked it again from the inside and suggested a change in repertoire. While he disinfected and washed all my clothes, I could use the bathroom strictly for staff where there was hot water and a tub. 'If you hear a knock on the door,' he said, 'get out immediately.' That proved to be unnecessary, fortunately, and so I had my first hot bath since arrival in the Gestapo camp while all my clothes were washed and disinfected.

Yet all the wet stuff had to be put on for the return to barrack 7. The wind was icy cold and, when I arrived, I crackled from head to foot. Room was made around the stove. Someone lent me an overcoat while all the clothes were hung on a piece of rope strung around the stovepipe.

While the surviving lice in my mattress planned their nocturnal assault, I reflected that night on the cruelty of a system which treated humans as dispensable ends and as items in a rulebook. Yet there had also been glimpses of Christian kindness, humour and compassion that day. And as long as they persevered, I felt the system would destroy itself, as indeed it did!

Part II
Magdeburg Prison

5

Bestiality

AT DAWN ON FRIDAY 14 JANUARY 1944, during the regular morning countdown, my name and that of my fellow felons were called out. We were not to march off with the crews that were sent to work that day. Three weeks of hard labour had begrimed me almost beyond recognition. There was no soap for washing or razor for shaving, my shoes and socks had gaping holes, I still had not been able to find buttons for my coat and shirt and there was no change of clothes or opportunity to clean what I had on. Any change was welcome.

When the working crews had left, the three of us left behind began to speculate. Were we going to be released? Were we going to be further interrogated (a frightening thought if the horrifying stories of fellow prisoners about additional interrogations were to be believed)? We quickly eliminated that idea. We had already confessed to our crime of spreading the BBC news. We settled for the most favourable possibility. The Gestapo had just wanted to teach us a lesson and now they were going to let us go. How wrong we were!

Finally, the officer on duty came around to where we stood.

'Get your gear and report to my office!' he barked.

That meant release, we concluded. Back we were in no time flat. Dish, blanket and metal cup were handed in, and we were eagerly ready for the next move. But no-one in the office was in a great hurry. Half-an-hour passed and still nothing. Finally, an officer opened a cupboard and handed us our confiscated possessions, wallets, pocketknives, passports, pocket dictionaries. Again nothing. We began to write postcards to our parents in the Netherlands saying that we were being released and that everything was OK now, but we never got the chance to post them.

At 10.00 a.m. the camp commandant appeared. He would take us to the Gestapo headquarters on the Regierungsstrasse, he said. We assumed that we would be released from there, possibly after a dressing down. Nothing could dampen our optimism!

Soon we left, walking down the muddy path, just the four of us. This time there were no heavily armed guards urging us on to march faster. We boarded a tram, but in downtown Magdeburg we had to change for another one that would take us to the Gestapo headquarters. It was at this tram stop that the commandant told us to wait. He had some errands to do. We were now more than ever convinced that soon we would be freed. Would the Gestapo leave us unguarded if it thought we were dangerous? Escaping — which we had often dreamt about — would be insane at this point, we felt.

And so we waited until the commandant reappeared from a restaurant where he had obviously enjoyed a cup of coffee. Later we were far less convinced that we had not been sharply watched during this interlude. Had the ever-suspicious Gestapo not actually set a trap to prove that our unbelievable guilelessness was not for real and that we were actually dangerous spies trained in sophisticated techniques of sabotaging the German war machinery?

At the Gestapo headquarters our hopes were utterly dashed. As if by magic all laxity vanished. The commandant disappeared in an office. Uniformed thugs took over, barked commands and ordered us around. I asked what I thought was a civil question. It might have been: 'Could I go to the bathroom, please?', but I have forgotten the details. What I certainly remember is the violence it unleashed. All of a sudden I had become the scum of the earth. I was slapped and pushed and thrown bodily into a dank, dark cell without any furniture. It was so dark that I could only feel my way around through touching the walls. I slouched in a corner in deepest despair.

It was this day I kept dreaming about for years afterwards. The sudden beastliness, the barbarous brutality, the violent irrational viciousness had caught me off guard. My coping mechanism was not up to it. The dreams always finished with a nightmare of being savagely attacked and beaten into pulp. Then I would wake up. They kept recurring for years afterwards until slowly and steadily my dreams reflected my taking the bashing in my stride. As soon as I would think, in my dream, 'Let them kill me, if that is what they want', the beating would stop and my sleep would continue restfully rather than my waking up in a bath of perspiration. The dream had the consequence that death held not much of a threat any longer. One reason that I like Arthur Koestler's *Darkness at Noon* so much is that the hero Rubasjow goes through a similar ordeal of imprisonment and similarly keeps having nightmares about it.

The experience had another consequence. From about this time I kept looking less for brilliance, wittiness and smartness in people than for the kind of depth which I instinctively felt would raise them above any ordeal that happened to strike them. I found it much less in the circles of intellectuals who were at the top of my totempole then, and much more amongst Christians at any level of the prestige scale. Not that I always found it there either, but at least with them and in the churches there were persistent pointers to what I began to dimly discover was meant by salvation, the source of depth, the kind of miraculous integrity which put ordeal and sin in perspective. The pointers began to focus more sharply on Jesus who, par excellence, incorporated that vision. I had always despised the cheap pictures of Jesus on the cross with a corona around his head, but now I began to discover the profoundness of the statement that he had conquered death and represented radiant, saving life more completely than humans did. But all these reflections and discoveries occurred much later.

Yet it was Gestapo brutality which triggered new understanding, new coping, new priorities, new faith. Freud, Marx, Nietzsche and other despisers of religion who are taken so seriously in my discipline — sociology of religion — would call these ripening convictions of mine 'projections of wishdreams', 'puerile resolutions of coping problems', 'unscientific extrapolations', 'unmanly thoughts of losers', 'crutches for the helpless'. I am not sure that any of them ever understood the depth of the very religion they were despising or that their own assumptions were at all inadequate. Neither, frankly, are the ideas of those philosophers or laymen for whom a God who allows Gestapo viciousness to persist is a nothing. As though man's barbarity and sin is *not* an existential 'given' and can be sent into oblivion with the stroke of a biro, clear thinking or the will of a robot ego! It is only when sin is conceived as a basic flaw in human nature that God's divine intervention in Jesus becomes the miracle it is. Only then can despair become a building block rather than a stumbling block. In Jesus, God revealed his salvation and this slowly began to mean to me that through participation in this saving event — 'being in Christ' — ordeals of any kind, including Gestapo bestiality, could be overcome and stowed away as important ingredients for solid integrity.

After half-an-hour or so I began to recover somewhat from the bestial treatment and take notice of my environment. The cell stank of excrement and vomit. No doubt it had housed time and again those who were recovering from bouts of interrogation. It was pitch dark, but touch and smell were enough to make my flesh creep. I crouched back in my corner, head between my knees, but this did little to relieve resurging despondency. I assumed that despair was exactly what the Gestapo intended me to feel. But why? We had all confessed to our crime of passing on the BBC news. Did the secret police suspect more?

The answer was soon to come. Two Gestapo officers in civil clothing unlocked our cells. Instead of dreaded interrogation, however, came another trip through town in a tram. We got out near the impressive court of justice. We had only been regarded as transients and the cell was the only place they could think of putting us until further transport could be arranged. But why the harsh treatment before we were pushed into the cell? We could only guess that all accused unfortunate enough to enter were given the same indiscriminate treatment.

The Magdeburg palace of justice, too, proved to be a temporary stop. We first imagined that we were to be tried, but the trial proved to be months ahead, as we discovered later. Additional information was all the court officials needed. In their haste the Gestapo had forgotten to get everything straight originally. The officers insisted that we face the wall while being questioned which was rather disconcerting. The questions were innocuous, however, and our violation of the broadcasting laws appeared to be the only charge against us.

Soon the formalities were over. Through a back door we entered the Magdeburg prison and this would prove to be 'our home' for the next six months. A prison guard made us strip and take a shower. All our dilapidated clothing was put in a box and instead we received an issue of prison garb: underclothing, blue trousers, blue jacket, socks and a pair of slippers without heels. It was all very clean and quite a change from the Gestapo camp. I kept slipping out of my slippers until after a few days I got the knack of keeping them on. Running in them was impossible: the intention was obviously to stop us fleeing.

Cleanliness, quiet and order struck me first when we entered the cell blocks. From the bottom all I could see were rows of doors entering on five floors, each with a narrow gallery extending along the entire length. The sun's rays came through a large window at the end where the stairs were. Some of the heavy copper locks on the cell doors glowed in refracted light. The varnished doors, the whitewashed walls and the polished linoleum reminded me of sickness and hospitals. There was a prisoner putting out earthen water jugs at each cell and behind him came a guard who, with much clanging, opened each door in turn. Out would come a little man — or so it seemed — who swiftly took the jug and was locked up again, clankety-clank. I remember how later as inmates we would be waiting for this moment just to see something different from four naked walls.

That first glimpse of prison stayed with me all my life: it was all so orderly and yet so infinitely depressing.

I was taken to cell 272 on the third floor, but stayed only ten minutes. The two inmates had cleverly managed to exchange a pullover for extra food — I am still mystified about the mechanics of this form of corruption — and obviously I would be in the way of the wheeling and dealing. And so I landed in cell 286.

It was unoccupied and I could without restraint lick the wounds which this Friday the fourteenth of January 1944 had been inflicted on my soul. It had been full of unexpected, disastrous turns which my young life had not encountered before. I had never felt so alone. Never before had I been so completely at the mercy of evil forces which had swamped me like a gale force. I was rudderless and the sense of having all studs kicked from underneath was bewildering. Asking reasonable questions about the why and what of things had been brusquely and unequivocally denied. The Gestapo treated any independent thought — even expressed in the form of a question — as a grave insult. All it would tolerate was mindless servility and silent compliance.

Then something strange happened: I cried out for my father. I had not done that before and have not done it since. He and I had never been very close. He was rather ineffectual, anything but a leader of men. He never expressed himself very well and carried his emotions on his sleeve. Yet he was quite intelligent and probably the most knowledgeable and administratively capable farmer in the district. He was always at peace with himself and never had a sleepless night in his life. He was certainly not a Christian. Very occasionally he would scoff at the irrationality of faith. And yet I had cried out for him. Why? One of these days I must ask one of my psychiatrist friends. For all it is worth, what I probably needed at that time was restoration of my wounded manliness, a rediscovery of acceptable authority, balance and control. And my father represented at least some of these for me.

It was after this episode that God's fatherhood became more relevant. Not just as a better symbol for order and integrity than my own less-than-perfect father represented. Nor as a crutch or psychological projection, essentially concocted to heal a bruised ego. Not even as the crucial model for authority and love which everybody carries as a lodestar for maturation after the practical experience of such models in childhood. No, it was all these things, but more important than any of them was the growing understanding of God's fatherhood as the fitting image of his essential being as creator, preserver and loving judge. God's fatherhood was the link with my essential being, but it also made the self, with its need for symbols of meaning, authority, love and maturation, less central. God's fatherhood diminished the self as the core of preoccupation and substituted an actual relationship for it. It was the latter which almost effortlessly provided the wholeness and cohesiveness which had escaped me while I was searching for it within myself.

6

My first cell mate

MY FIRST CELL MATE IN the Magdeburg prison was in his sixties and could have been my grandfather. He had stolen tobacco out of parcels he was supposed to sort in the post office. He was a lonely bachelor without friends. Life had passed him by and I felt pity for him. He had grown up in Magdeburg, but his parents had died and his sisters had moved away. He lived in a boarding house and, apart from the daily cups of coffee, a pipe had been his main source of pleasure. Yet good tobacco was difficult to come by. The rationed stuff in the shop, he kept telling me, was very inferior and so the temptation to steal the high quality tobacco in the Red Cross parcels had been too much. He had been caught red-handed and now he was in this miserable cell where he could not smoke at all, not even the inferior brands he had to put up with in war-time Germany. He was very sorry for himself.

German prisons were overcrowded. The cell we were in was only two by three metres and originally intended for one prisoner only. There was one bed which during the day could be folded against the wall. If more prisoners were brought in, they had to sleep on mattresses filled with woodshavings. They were stacked in the corner and were spread out in the evening. At one time four of us had to share a one-person cell and the whole floor was covered that night.

I had been the first in cell 286 and so the bed was mine by rights of seniority. However, I felt sorry for the old man and said that I had no objection to sleeping on the floor. Unfortunately, the woodshavings in the mattress had clustered in five moist lumps and after the first night's sleep, or lack of it, I began to somewhat regret my generosity. But by then it was too late.

My kindness was interpreted as deference to the German master race. The Dutch and Scandinavians were treated relatively well compared with foreigners from eastern countries, but even they were several notches below the exalted, destined-for-glory 'Herrenvolk', in the estimation of my cell mate. He was not a member of the Nazi party, but the glorification of the nation appealed to all. Hitler had managed to rally the entire country behind the war effort and the German military superiority in the first half of World War II gave pride to young and old alike. There was nothing faintly reminiscent of the master race in the bloodless, dreary old man, but I felt it was not my job to disillusion him. The 'virility' illusion gave him a certain measure of self-respect.

In the prison, foreigners had to wear a big 'A' standing for *Auslander* sewn on the front of their jackets, so it was not difficult to discover that as many as three-quarters of prisoners in our section were non-Germans. They were carefully mixed. Compatriots were never put together and political prisoners were usually separated from one another. This meant that in Magdeburg at any rate I was hardly ever in a cell with another Dutchman or with another anti-Nazi. If there were too many political prisoners and some of them had to be put together, the authorities made sure at least that the nationalities were thoroughly mixed.

There were two good reasons for this policy. The Germans were acutely conscious of their unpopularity with the subjugated nations and they feared conspiracies even when they did not exist. It was essential for them to separate actual or potential enemies or, if that were impossible, to keep them under constant surveillance by well-oiled, well-informed secret police. But just as important was German solidarity which the Goebbels propaganda machine persistently and forcefully bolstered through setting the nation off against others. Before the outbreak of World War II, the Jews had served this purpose. They continued to be at the bottom of the heap, but there were now few left and a whole array of new scapegoats had to take their place in order to strengthen the boundary around heart-warming, blood-stirring nationalism. The 'A' on our jackets served that purpose as admirably as the David star on Jewish coats, or the tirades against the American and British plutocrats.

Apart from tobacco, patriotism had become the religion of my cell mate. Goebbels had fully succeeded with him. The glory of the nation was the banner under which his old heart rallied. I made no attempt to convince him otherwise. It would have been wasted effort. To me, German patriotism was unadulterated evil. It had led to the inhumanity which I had witnessed and of which I was the victim. Yet my cell mate fully approved of the atrocities I told him about. Invariably he would say that it was all very sad, but then he would add that the war effort made it all necessary and that our suffering was modest compared with that of the heroic soldiers dying at the front. Given these convictions, he felt that my violation of the broadcasting laws was a heinous crime, much worse than his stealing tobacco destined for what were, after all, only foreigners.

German nationalism was demonic because it squashed humanness. But then this very 'humanness' could, given a chance, become just as logically and inevitably demonic. The religious fervour in the West surrounding self-realisation, self-affirmation and self-assertion is as impregnable for many as nationalism was for my old cell mate. It can be equally demonic in that it can and does subvert the common good and make shambles of the collective effort, whether focussed on the family, the community, the nation or internationalism. Narcissism — a morbid, exclusive concern with selfhood — can be as monstrous as nationalism — a morbid, exclusive concern with a nation. Both are prone to make a sliver of reality a divine, all-encompassing, all-determining authority.

At any rate, my German cell mate gave me a glimpse of what deeply motivated the nation. I did not like it, but it did open my eyes to the other forms of idolatry endangering other nations and peoples, including myself. It gave me an entirely new appreciation of Christianity as the harbinger of a truth transcending, yet also somehow accepting, all man's narrow loyalties to himself, his family, his community, his nation.

My first cell mate also proved to be a homosexual. At first his advances were so subtle and hesitant that they escaped my attention. When they became less ambiguous and I finally latched on to their meaning, I felt pity rather than repulsion.

In my sheltered life I had never met homosexuals before. I guess I could have found them earlier if my not insubstantial libido had been more congenial to what nowadays is euphemistically called 'this particular sexual preference'. Both then and now the physical, or anal, part of the homosexual relationship seemed to me peculiarly inappropriate. I had always visualised (I was a 'virgin' then) that a penis and a vagina were most fittingly, pleasantly and beautifully fashioned for one another and that together they were incomparable for procreation and for mutual fulfilment and completion.

My cell mate made the advance after the light was turned out. We were still sitting at the table munching on our dry slice of bread before turning in for the night. His hand strayed to my thigh and crotch. I did what millions of women have done instinctively: I took his hand, put it back on his own thigh and moved over slightly. Feeling his embarrassment, I helped him get over it by directing the discussion to his favourite topic, the might of the German army. The gesture had been so pathetic, his vulnerability so aching and pitiable, his loneliness and anxiety so telling, that I wanted him to be assured of my goodwill and sympathy. Not, however, any sexual interest!

I have often wondered whether I could have handled the

situation better by addressing the issue head on rather than by evasion. However, in those days my sexual feelings were still a problem to me, although malnutrition had already begun to mercifully muffle them. I could not possibly and dispassionately have discussed those of someone else — let alone an older person — without either being a hypocrite or by making a fool of myself. Neither was I then Christian enough to think about sexuality in the wider and glowing perspective of faith.

Nazism and the German Army feared homosexuality as unadulterated vileness. Later in another cell block at Magdeburg I met soldiers who had received harsh sentences for homosexual advances. The propaganda machine of the army pictured the soldier as aggressively masculine and lustily heterosexual. Shortly before my liberation at the Dutch border in April 1945, I met hundreds of twittering, buxom German teenage girls — they were called 'grey mice' because of the colour of their uniforms — coming out of a military freight train. Their job had been to 'entertain' the troops and to keep their heterosexual interests alive.

The prison population had similar feelings about homosexuality. A thief had higher status than a'queer'. Some other sexual deviants, however, were received rather well. During one of the air-raids on Magdeburg when the inhabitants of the cells on the top floor were squeezed into the bottom one, I met a man of seventy-four who happily and unashamedly explained to all and sundry that he had produced a child by his daughter-in-law. The son had been less than happy about the unexpected addition to the family when he arrived back on furlough from the Russian front and had gone to the police. The old man had been given a gaol sentence to cool his ardour. The story impressed other inmates and so he was one of the few non-political prisoners who freely discussed his misdemeanour.

7

Discipline

THE GERMAN WAR MACHINE was a sight for sore eyes. Dynamism with a purpose had always intrigued me and one had to be blind not to find it the very moment one set foot in Germany during World War II. The hopelessness of the depression and the tiredness of the urban proletariat had vanished as if by magic. Now there was a common purpose to which all the ill-used, smouldering vitality could be directed. Germany was to be the queen of nations, no other country matching its power. To explain the horrors of Nazi Germany as the outcome of Hitler's power-crazy, insane mind is ever so much rubbish. Germany and Hitler drew power from each other and even the stated goal of national supremacy was less important than the hidden role of the war to replace meaninglessness with meaning, dissipation with loyalty, self-pity with self-sacrifice, demoralising unemployment with fulfilling work.

It was labour, hard labour, which fuelled the German war-machine and all institutions — including the extensive prison system — had to fit the need for workers. And so already on my second day in the Magdeburg prison at eight in the morning, two thousand sheets of cardboard and paper were brought in. My cell mate and I were shown how to fold the cardboard and cover it with pre-printed sheets so that the resulting box could be filled with washing powder in a factory.

'Unless you make fifteen hundred today,' the guard said,

'you will get less bread tonight.' Now the existing ration was much below what was needed to still our hunger and so we worked as hard as we could. But it was all in vain. By six o'clock in the evening we had not even managed to produce eight hundred and we waited with trepidation for the evening hand-out of the dry slice of bread. Would they halve it, leaving us with about seventy-five grams, about five mouthfuls? Fortunately, we received the full ration and we learnt later that no one ever made the full quota of washing powder packets, covers for aspirin jars, paper bags, brooms or whatever to be manufactured. As long as there was no loafing on the job, the prison officials saw no reason to increase our malnutrition below the danger level. They aimed at maximum output for minimum nutriment, but realised soon enough that below that minimum the amount of work would steeply drop.

One day a heavy-set Belgian butcher came to join us. He had worked in a downtown butcher's shop, but had been caught selling meat without ration coupons for an exorbitant price. He felt — and acted! — like a caged animal, pacing up and down, flailing his arms and his agitation soon began to have an effect on all of us. His big fingers were not used to delicate paperwork and the total output for that day was less than the day before when there had been only two of us. The guard in charge of the work detail soon moved him out and put him on the quarry crew, a group of prisoners who were made to cut and cart stone all day somewhere on the edge of Magdeburg. We saw him a few weeks later in the exercise yard. His face was hollow and his body had become that of a walking skeleton. The quarry prisoners usually did not last long. Underfed bodies could not cope with the hard work, and dust ruined the lungs.

Other prisoners were much better off. They were put to work in the bakery, the bookbinder's, the shoemaker's and the blacksmith's shops, all within the prison walls. They received extra bread and soup and had the great advantage of more breathing space. Instead of being cooped up between four cell walls, they could move around and practise their trade. They were usually prisoners who had been sentenced. In our section of the prison, however, almost all inmates were still awaiting trial.

Of those who had not had their court cases yet, the political prisoners were put at a deliberate disadvantage. The criminals sometimes managed to become 'kallifactors', cleaners of corridors and toilet pots or, even better, food distributors. But this never happened to those, such as my friends and I, who had committed anti-Nazi crimes! In the prison hierarchy the Nazi guards had assigned us to the lowest rung. By contrast, they allowed the criminals to nominate their underworld friends for various housekeeping jobs. All this led to a corrupt chain of rewards for small favours from which intellectuals and politicals were firmly excluded.

Yet work had its own intrinsic rewards. Those whom the Gestapo had singled out as national solidarity risks actually had an advantage in that they had usually more psychological stamina. They had stood up for what they felt was inherently true or right in spite of propaganda lies and censor's distortions. Mental pluck had a built-in survival benefit: it bolstered independence from the social setting. Political prisoners could be loners if need be and some of them used work as a support for self-confidence rather than for social purposes. I liked even humdrum work. It helped to keep the wolf of dissolution away. The rhythm and the ritual of work somehow strengthened whatever little self-respect I had left in those early days. Ever since, I have been conscious of the deeply destabilizing effect of unemployment. Financial compensation, however adequate, does not even begin to make up for the absence of meaningful or even humdrum work. A sense of accomplishment and self-worth has to rest on something rather concrete.

Yet work is only an aid to, rather than the source of, integrity and morale. It helped me to regain my bearings, rather than establish a solid foundation for the future. Work in the prison at the time was a useful way of forgetting and escaping from the pain of confinement. Only much later did it become for me an integral part of God's destiny as he in his wisdom had plotted it for me.

Work was in no way the only source of discipline in the German prison system. Salvation through discipline in any possible form was clearly the underlying rationale of what it was all about. And the guards fell in enthusiastically behind the fetish for promptness and military precision. They felt that they should be at the front fighting for Germany's honour, but seeing that they were either too old or too decrepit for this more exalted form of service, they settled for the next best thing: a miniature army within prison walls. In this game we were the dumb recruits and they were the drill sergeants. Thought was out, performance in. Unless the place ran like clockwork, they felt incurably insecure and close to mental collapse.

And so the day was neatly cut in half with six in the morning and six in the evening the ordained divisions between night and day. The light was promptly turned on at 6.00 a.m. and turned off as close as possible to 6.00 p.m. Now the latter hour was a bit awkward as someone in the hierarchy had perversely determined that 6.00 p.m. was also to be the moment for the evening meal, one hundred and fifty grams of dry bread. But then prisoners could learn to do things in the dark. After all, the soldiers on the front did not have light bulbs to eat by and the prison was not supposed to be like a hotel anyway. Fortunately, the guard in command had to finish the feeding of his row of cells before he could begin switching lights. And so we usually had a few minutes' grace in which we could actually see what we were eating. Undressing, by contrast, took place unfailingly and unwantonly in the dark.

But I am running ahead of myself. The mornings began with the naked bulb staring in one's eyes and were followed briskly by dressing, stacking mattresses, rinsing one's face, pouring the dirty water in the portable toilet in the corner and waiting for the guard. His coming was announced by the big key turning twice in the lock and by the bolt being removed. Unless we were there ready to put out the empty water jug and the filled and chastely covered toilet pot, the guard would colourfully and ear-shatteringly chew us out.

This phase of the morning ritual being accomplished, we could relax for a minute until the trusties outside had filled the jug and emptied the pot. Then there was another moment for which supreme alertness was required. The jug and the pot had to be hauled inside while the guard counted the seconds between opening and closing of cell doors. The law of survival dictated that the most nimble-fingered inmate would handle whatever was filled and the more clumsy ones whatever was empty. Yet nimbleness was no use, unless one could also avoid tripping over one another during the momentary traffic congestion in the door opening.

One day in the cell next door two inmates collided. The carrier of the full toilet bowl went sprawling, still clutching the vessel. The contents, however, spilled over the corridor and down to the main floor below. Worse than the stench and the personal discomfort was the guard who for as long as it took to clean the mess practised his remarkable range of invectives and expletives at the top of his voice. He happened to be an aesthete at heart and refused to repeat himself more than twice. To our startled surprise, he began to use French swearwords when his German vocabulary had run out. I wondered afterwards whether he would have started on other foreign swear words, which he had obviously picked up from his polyglot charges, if the clean-up had not finished there and then.

Seven o'clock was spit-and-polish time. The hour actually began with breakfast, but there was so little of it that in practice it turned out to be but a minor interlude. All the inmates of the cell had to line up against the wall between two cell doors with heels meeting and eyes straight ahead. Half a litre of brown hot water — it was supposed to be coffee, but one could hardly tell from the taste — was ladled in the dish we held right in front. With the other hand we received one hundred and fifty grams of dry bread. It only took a minute or so to wolf it down and then the cell cleaning could begin.

There was very little tidying to do, but what there was had to gleam. Every day, the cover of the lavatory pot, the dustpan and the washbasin had to be rubbed with red sand until they shone. The floor had to be swept, scrubbed and polished and the guard made sure that not a single corner was passed by. Nothing much escaped his eagle eye and he received perverse satisfaction out of detecting neglected details. We on the other hand felt good when the cell passed muster, not so much because we had dodged an ear-bashing, but because we had lived up to expectations of cleanliness.

In retrospect it seems strange that those of us who had so actively opposed German militarism and for whom the mind-numbing spit-and-polish exercise every day was a cunning way of coercing us back into infantile obedience, nevertheless took pride in brightening our little environment and felt warmed by the guard's praise. Did we relive the simple childhood rewards of approval when the teacher liked the neatness of our exercise book and parents commended our shoe-polishing? Or was it that we had no choice and that coercion had the desired effect of making us into cooperative conformists?

Strangely enough, having no choice appealed to at least some of my fellow-inmates, however much they also missed their freedom. To them prison was a welcome retreat to the simple life they remembered from childhood. Regimentation meant absence of responsibility, evasion of the frictions inevitable in any working environment and the raising of a family, avoidance of the harsh judgements of an achievement-orientated society. This was not true for me. I loathed mindless regimentation and relished responsibility. Yet to me, too, there was a certain satisfaction in the return to the simplest of conditions or, better, in the capacity to make something positive out of what seemed nothing but outright disaster.

Almost anything of value before imprisonment — family,

food, freedom, friends, books, job, music — was taken away
or reduced. Could something be made out of what was left?
It was startling to discover that indeed a new world could be
built on the ruins of an old one, provided one had a foundation. Then new satisfactions could be created out of previously ignored elements: a crust of bread, a well-polished
washbasin, approval of an illiterate guard, the memories of
a cell mate from the underworld, the half-dead remainder of
a dahlia in the exercise yard, one's hopes for the defeat of
Nazism.

There was one big difference: that new world was
extremely simple. It was as though the old world had been
stripped of layer upon layer of trivial ingredients until
nothing much seemed left. Yet what was left proved to be of
great value precisely because it was so elemental. Later it
began to dawn that it was this foundation which the preacher
of my Dutch village church had called Jesus Christ. He had
always insisted that Christ was the cornerstone upon which
the new house of faith and interpretation could be erected.
I had to become impossibly poor — the prison stripped away
all securities — in order to discover the richness of Christ
who for our sakes became poor that we through his poverty
might be rich.

As a teenager this truth had escaped me altogether. Now,
being deprived of all these layers of skin-deep certainty, I
slowly re-discovered what long ago St Paul, St Augustine,
Bunyan, Tolstoy and many others had found: that ' the simplicity that is in Christ' was like a rock on which a fuller life
could be built. The military claptrap, which my sense of
humour put in its proper place, and the elimination of
mundane certitude, which forced me to find a new source of
confidence, helped to generate this simple trust and elemental faith in Christ the Saviour. And he proved, and proves in
final resort, to be the firmest foundation for a new world.

8

Escape

DURING THE MORNING OF 17 JANUARY 1944 a guard
came into our cell: 286. We jumped up and stood at attention.
He looked us over from head to foot. Then he turned to my
old cell mate and, with a voice that carried beyond the prison
walls, chewed him out for his dishevelled appearance. His
authority now firmly emblazoned on our souls, he turned to
me and shouted, 'Get out!'

I followed him down the corridor, down the stairs, round
one corner and down another passage into an office. He
clicked his heels and raised the Hitler salute, but the portly
man behind the empty desk took scant note. The guard being
dismissed, the middle-aged gentleman introduced himself as
the examining magistrate. He offered me a chair and asked:

'Where did you get the radio for listening to the BBC?'

'We bought it secondhand in Kleinwanzleben. It did not
work, but we fixed it.'

'Why did you listen to the station of the lying plutocrats?'

'We tried to get the Dutch news and sometimes strayed to
other channels.'

'How did you manage to pass the information to the
French and Russian prisoners of war?'

'We worked with them. They could not read German, nor
did they have access to a radio. Yet they were keen to get
news about the front.'

So he went on for another half-hour. I gave him the
answers which fitted with the way my friends and I had

agreed the story should be presented: innocent dialling on our radio set and listening to whatever language we could understand. We had decided to allay any suspicion that we were out to wreck the German war-machine. We had already confessed to the lesser crime and the Gestapo had failed to find the anti-Nazi leaflets I had managed to destroy.

Finally, he asked whether I had any questions.

'When will the trial be?'

'The courts are clogged. I don't think that your case will come up in the next few months.'

'What kind of sentence is meted out on average for our misdemeanour?'

'The courts take a serious view of offences against the broadcasting laws.'

He was obviously aware that I had not adjusted well to the sudden change in fortunes: from relative freedom and sufficient food to imprisonment and gnawing hunger.

'However, you yourself can shorten the waiting period considerably.'

He saw my sad and thin face light up.

'If I were in your shoes I would join the Waffen SS. This would prove to the court that you are not *Deutschfeindlich*, hostile to the German cause. You would be freed almost immediately. The trial would be advanced and your sentence postponed, more likely cancelled. I have the forms here. All you have to do is sign.'

Unfortunately, he was not in my shoes! Nor could he imagine that what was obviously good for Germany was by definition bad for all the nations its armies conquered. He assumed that Hitler's armies were going to civilise the world and therefore all well-thinking human beings would naturally come aboard!

I did not feel it was my job to change his mind. There was no chance for that anyway! We lived in two separate worlds. But his world had all the cards and I had none. And so I gave a non-committal answer.

'Well,' came his reply, 'the warden has the same forms. If

you decide to join the glorious battle with the enemies of the Reich, he will assist you in every possible way.'

Then I was free to go. It had happened before that we had been invited to join the Waffen SS. At the time — during our time in the Gestapo camp — my friends and I had made fun of the fellow prisoner who had gone around with a list for signatures of volunteers. Poking fun at such an invitation was now impossible. Joining was now linked with our court case: it was proof that we were not hostile to the German war effort and not joining was proof that we were. Listening to the BBC, like refusing to accept an invitation to join the Waffen SS, was to the examining magistrate, and later to the lawyers and the judges, clear evidence of our 'Deutschfeindlichkeit', which of course it was!

Later, in June 1944, a third attempt was made to entice me into the Waffen SS. This time it was the warden himself who summoned me.

'Where were you born?'

'In Rosenburg.' Even a superficial perusal of my file could have given him that information — so it was obviously an opener for more serious things to come.

'Rosenburg, Germany?'

'No, Rosenburg, Holland.' I should have been flattered that my German was so good that I had passed for a German, but I wasn't.

'Well, I was wondering whether you would be interested in joining the Waffen SS. They need you badly on the front and your prison term would be cancelled.'

On this occasion I was even more emaciated and in a correspondingly poor frame of mind. I also had to avoid having a sentence added for continued hostility to the German war effort. Similarly, I had to avoid the risk of being sent to a concentration camp after the prison term. I had been coughing blood, and so I used that as an excuse for being less than interested. Hopefully, the Waffen SS was not so hard up that it pressured young people with tuberculosis to join up!

And that is where the matter came to rest. Or did it? I had

begun to despair of surviving the ordeal. Allied successes and dreaming about escape had so far kept hopes alive. They provided the psychological stamina to endure. There was nothing one could do about the defeat of Germany. But dreaming about escape gave me a constant and much needed lift.

Yet plots could only go so far. They had to be implemented. Later that year during the transfer to Halle I managed to keep my passport, though at the considerable risk of discovery. This was important, as in the free world one needed identification for almost anything. On arrival at the prison in Halle other prisoners and I had to get out of our civilian clothes on one side of a large room and walk in the nude to the other side for the hand-out of prison garb. Yet I had managed to clutch my passport without being spotted. So far so good.

But there were other, more formidable obstacles. The wall separating the street from the factory where the contingent of prisoners worked could be scaled. But in less than half-an-hour the guard would discover my absence and would sound the alarm. Only with help could I get civilian clothes and be out of Halle before detection. The opportunity never came.

Maybe it was all to the good. Hardly anyone ever escaped and those who did were soon caught, paraded before us and executed. Yet the thought crossed my mind that the opportunity for escaping would advance greatly if I were to sign the Waffen SS form. Why not be Machiavellian? The entire Nazi world surrounding me encouraged the brutal principle of means serving the end. Supremacy of the master race and survival at any cost were the dogmas of Nazism. Why not use the SS for my own escape and survival? I felt sorely tempted, but something held me back.

It probably was a sense of principle which won out over Machiavellism. The prison had torn much to shreds. Yet a stubborn sense of what I felt I stood for was still intact at the time. If anything, Gestapo treatment had strengthened the resolve to remain true to my Dutch origins, to a belief in democracy, to abhorrence of Nazism and to the values of compassion, reason and respect for human beings. Going the path of joining the SS, even if only to escape, would lead to a self-loathing worse than physical suffering. In prison I could at least live with myself.

Yet weakening integrity was the problem for young people of my age. Most of us were still growing up. We were still groping for our niche in spite of brave fronts. How could the remaining sense of self, which seemed as precarious as health and freedom, be strengthened? If it went, all was lost. So much had already gone: the security of home and friends, independent action, a taken-for-granted status. And so the SS proposal was rejected.

But only after an internal struggle. Integrity versus opportunism. I was brought up to use opportunities well. The Great Depression had seen to that! The imprisonment had made us even more expert in taking advantage of any chance for an extra ounce of bread or an easier job. From the vantage point of today, the school of hard knocks had made us much more adroit at exploiting potential than our children and grandchildren will ever be.

Yet there was a limit. Instinctively I had stopped at opportunism as a mainspring of action, as the underlying motive for surviving. Integrity was not to be subsumed under whimsy. Mastery and survival at any price offended something in me that had been part of my upbringing. Yet it was unarticulated, vague and tantalisingly elusive, so much so that at one stage, which I will mention later on, it left me altogether. What was it?

I had never thought about it much. Young people never do. It had something to do with values and beliefs which I took for granted. Yet, if I were to survive this ordeal, it was important to gain some clarity about these values and beliefs. Otherwise they might very well be sucked down in the dizzy round of disasters choking whatever little was left of my sense of identity.

I did not solve the problem of integrity versus opportunism

then. Yet the invitations to join the Waffen SS and the perpetual plots for escape compelled me to take stock. Where was I heading? Which beliefs and values determined both what I was and what I should be? If integrity was as crucial as I was slowly and painfully discovering it to be, how could it be preserved and strengthened? The search was on.

It eventually culminated in the conviction that I was anything but alone. There were other fellow prisoners whose opportunism was constrained by integrity. I was to meet some of them later that year. More importantly, there was an enormous crowd of witnesses in Christian history who had paved a highway where, in my insufferable arrogance and blindness, I had only seen an impenetrable wilderness!

Jesus, for one, in his young life had rejected opportunism personified by Satan in the wilderness and had accepted the verdict that man should live by something more than bread. And wasn't Christ's crucifixion actually his choice for integrity rather than the sham world of hypocritical clerics and Machiavellian conquerors? Well, what was good enough for Christ and hosts of followers down the ages should certainly be sufficient for puny me! Yet I had to suffer much more before this would become clearly established in my mind. And it took even longer for it to become an integral part of my strongly held convictions.

9

Air attack

TOWARDS THE END OF JANUARY 1944, Magdeburg
suffered its first air attack. It was late at night and the
deafening noise of bombs falling close to the prison woke us
with a jolt. As we took the black covering from our barred
window, the cell was aglow with the weird dancing light of
the fires. It made my German cell mates very nervous. The
lifeless old bachelor who had ransacked Red Cross parcels
for tobacco became extremely agitated.

He infected the other cell mate, a carpenter, who said he
was in prison because he had accused the Nazis of ruining his
construction firm when he refused to join them. The story
seemed plausible enough. After Hitler had come to power,
the population had become increasingly hesitant to support
those whom the party boycotted. And so after 1933 the
flourishing enterprise had declined drastically. Things had
gone from bad to worse when he had spurned a woman who
had dreamt of marrying him. Her fury had known no bounds.
She had made a nuisance of herself at the Gestapo headquarters and the Gestapo had finally concocted an indictable
offence to get rid of her pestering presence. He, too, was
scared out of his wits by the bombing.

The fireworks and explosions were indeed frightening. Yet
my cell mates puzzled me. Both acted so out of keeping with
their normal character. I had never thought of myself or my
family as phlegmatic; we were, if anything, a 'heart-on-one's
sleeve' family. Yet my reaction to imminent danger was

almost the reverse of theirs. I had learnt to rein in emotions when it really mattered, but to let go on almost any other occasion. And so my attempt to calm things down met with no success. They were almost three times my age and to take gaff from any foreigner was beneath the dignity of any German!

The carpenter, particularly, had seemed such a decent, stubborn old codger, and here he was exploding with fear. Ever since his arrival in our cell he had vexed us with dismal predictions about gas and germ warfare. The grim forebodings had been illustrations of a self-invented religion which rather unimaginatively began and ended with *Schicksal*, or fate. Yet at the first sign of his own scenario possibly becoming true, he had withered! His 'religion' could not be much of a motivating force, if he acted like this!

In other cells the air attack had apparently the same spine-chilling effect. Sporadic, anguished shouts welled up. Then the chorus began to swell eerily. Never before or since have I heard something as deeply disturbing as this common expression of helplessness of locked-up males. It was primordial and inhuman. They were caged animals and the primeval impulse of howling when life was at stake had penetrated all levels of culture and civilisation.

Then someone had the bright idea of augmenting the noise by pounding the steel with a hand brush, a standard piece of equipment in each cell. Others followed suit. The noise became deafening, far outstripping the explosions outside. My cell joined in the din with enthusiasm; it happily diverted the attention from bombs. It reminded me of the brushfires that firefighters purposely light to control the larger inferno. And it seemed to be just as effective; grave personal anxiety turned into something more salutary: concerted bedlam.

Bedlam it was, both inside and out. The few guards on night duty shouted commands to stop the racket, but no-one took note. They obviously felt that the heavy cell doors were their best ally for containing the seething, but separated mass. And so it was. After a while door beatings began to acquire a rhythm of their own. The pandemonium became an ordered, even ritualised expression of common fear. Yet it was the sense of being in this together which was the effective antidote to the primeval cry of personal helplessness.

The hand brush rumble stopped when the bombing did. Everyone went back to bunks and mattresses and soon my cell mates were fast asleep. The prison authorities did not want a repeat performance and in typical, thorough fashion devised plans in case there was another attack.

From now onwards the two top floors of the prison were evacuated as soon as the siren sounded and the prisoners were billeted in the corresponding cells on the lower two floors. The argument was that incendiary bombs would only penetrate the top floors, thereby allowing evacuation of the entire prison without too much loss of life. Actually only air-raid shelters could offer any protection, but the prison did not even have proper cellars. Still, the prisoners were happy with the new arrangement and there was no shouting and pounding when a few days later the next attack took place. Instead, everyone filed out in orderly fashion.

Downstairs we were locked in with the inhabitants of cell 86, two floors below us. They were all hardened criminals belonging to a work crew which marched out every day to Hubbe, a margarine factory. Although they were heavily guarded all day, they worked together with civilians and were able to snatch snippets of information about the war effort.

On the other hand we were completely cut off from the outside world and were actually very pleased to see new faces. To be cooped up with two elderly Germans whose range of interests was very narrow had not been particularly exhilarating for me. And so I plied them with questions: What had happened on the front? Who was retreating where? What was it like to be on a prison crew? How was the food? Was the work heavy? They were happy to give perfunctory answers, but for them the real excitement lay in their pilfering exploits.

They had just managed to put their hands on fifty packets of lard and exchanged them for a pouch of tobacco, a very valuable commodity on the prison market. Some of the tobacco in turn had been exchanged for food with those in charge of food distribution. They explained that all this required real proficiency. Once outside they saw a golden future for themselves. Pulling off robberies and burglaries would be child's play compared with what they had just managed under much more difficult conditions!

We were supposed to listen with open-mouthed admiration. I guess we did, but little did they know that what they thought was acclaim was actually surprise about their morality. At any rate they liked us for being good listeners and we liked them for their knowledge of the outside world. Through it all we had forgotten about the air-raid and we were actually sorry when we had to return to our own cells!

Air-raid warnings became a regular feature. Usually the planes would just fly over Magdeburg to Berlin. The incessant roar of their engines was invariably music to my ears. It was a most welcome reminder that the allies were now strong enough to penetrate deep into the German heartland. Their noise strengthened morale: suffering was being vindicated. I suppose that my cell mates reacted so differently because they did not have the benefit of identifying the attackers with angels of liberation!

Air-raid warnings also played havoc with the rule that nationalities should be mixed and that political prisoners should be separated. Soon the German carpenter was replaced by a Frenchman who said he had been caught at the border with stolen ashtrays. He was a mine of information about other prisons between Magdeburg and France and we drew the conclusion that we were comparatively well off. The Frenchman's German was non-existent, so I spent all day translating whatever the German cell mate wanted to communicate and vice-versa. Not that they had much in common. The Frenchman was devious and given to wild gesticulations; the German was dour and dull.

The next air-raid warning brought respite from constant translation. The cell downstairs had also changed personnel and it so happened that on this occasion all of us could jabber in our native tongues. The Dutchman was a shoemaker with a rather lengthy prison record about which he expressed neither pride nor regret. He had almost served his sentence and was in an expansive mood. Yes, he was quite happy to take a letter to my parents. Yes, he would nail it between the soles of his shoe. By this time I had become rather careful: I did not write anything that a censor could take exception to and I am glad I did. The letter never arrived and might very well have been used to curry favour for an informant. We had learnt to distrust intentions of criminals, particularly when they did not owe us anything. Often older compatriots who had volunteered for work in Germany had their reasons for feeling uncomfortable in their own communities. A criminal past or pro-Nazi sentiment easily brought on the kind of tension for which work in Germany was a happy solution.

Air-raids became a way of life all through 1944, particularly in Magdeburg where the prison received a direct hit later that year after we had been transferred to Halle. I always wondered how many inmates were killed on that occasion and whether the prison authorities managed to control the surviving ones. Was there an opportunity to escape, as all prisoners constantly dream about?

The air attacks helped us to come to grips with the possibility of sudden death. The prison was well built, yet a direct hit would kill large numbers. We were sitting ducks, all in our own little holes in the wall, securely locked up. The awful hammering of hundreds of hand brushes belting cell doors that first night represented a common fear of death. Its mournfulness had actually suggested the agony of dying. Even those with little imagination began to incorporate dying into their thinking about the future. Many repressed the thought, but others started to face it. I was amongst the latter.

The more I saw people dying, the more I wanted it to be

more than a meaningless event, the breakup of a physical system. I began to take note of those who saw themselves in a larger context. To them both life and death were part of an all-encompassing purpose, sometimes expressed in Christian language — 'being in God's hands' — but more often in such secular terms as dying for one's country or an ideal.

It was the larger context, I slowly learnt, which cushioned the shock of the unexpected and stopped emotional drainage. The larger context prepared the way for accepting the inevitable, death. Paul the apostle's statement that neither death nor life could separate us from the love of God had gone in one ear and out the other when I was a teenager. Now the profundity of it began to dawn. Life and death were real issues. The possibility of one turning into the other at the drop of a hat had become stronger and stronger.

That being the case, the raw fear of my cell mates during the first raid and my own sense of being completely at the mercy of the war events and Nazi thugs nurtured the search. Yet it was not so much an intellectual exercise as one of ripening conviction; not a reasoning, but a trusting. Faith was to grow slowly, but also inexorably, until many years later the full majesty of Paul's utterance that neither death nor life could separate me from God's love was understood in its entirety. Death then lost its sting!

10

The trial

ANY KIND OF MAIL WAS WELCOME, even the summons I received from the *Sondergericht* or Special Court on the last Saturday of March 1944! The *Sondergericht* was a special tribunal for political offenders, infamous for its ruthlessness, and the grapevine whispered that it sentenced prisoners to death on the flimsiest of evidence. Only judges and lawyers with long and impeccable records of service to the Party were allegedly allowed to serve on its exalted benches!

The letter was welcome in spite of its contents. Three months of starvation and uncertainty had taken its toll. Even a heavy sentence, we felt, was better than not knowing what to expect, and so I opened the letter with a sigh of relief. At least we had been spared the agony of rotting in a forgotten corner as appeared the case with some fellow prisoners who were still waiting for their day in court after more than a year.

In the summons the clerk of the court soon came to the point. We were charged with endangering the vital capacity of the German people to resist the enemy by purposely listening to the *Hetzesender* — hooligan radio station — in London and by purposely spreading its news. The clerk went on to say that the evidence was contained both in our own confessions and in the information received from the *Sonderdienst* — special Gestapo service — in Seehausen, a town not far from Kleinwanzleben and Magdeburg.

It was the first time I heard about the *Sonderdienst* and I imagined it to be the nerve centre for Gestapo spying on the civil population of the region. During the trial the *Sonderdienst* was carefully ignored. I assumed that the network of informers had to be shielded at any cost. For that reason, too, there were no witnesses. The population had to remain ignorant of whom it could trust or distrust.

That same afternoon my lawyer appeared. At considerable expense of time and effort I had finally managed to obtain his services. No one, least of all prison officials, wanted to assist political prisoners. Contamination was widely feared! Ostracism alone was safe. Even elementary kindness might be misconstrued as being in league with the enemy, so the prison authorities refused my request to help me get a lawyer. The boss of the factory administration under whom I had worked at Kleinwanzleben also ignored my plea to arrange for legal representation, as did the Lutheran prison chaplain. In desperation I sacrificed the rare letter I was allowed to send to my parents and instead wrote to a lawyer in downtown Magdeburg. He had been highly recommended by fellow prisoners.

This time I made a hit. He consented to represent me after being authorized by the prosecutor. I didn't know at the time that the special tribunal had to approve both a lawyer's visit to the accused and his defence. My attorney apparently had no trouble getting the permit and I soon discovered why. He was a notorious Nazi and his first words were that he had no sympathy for foreigners and particularly those who had committed a political offence. This took me aback, but I soon realised that it was better to get any lawyer than none at all. Later I met attorneys who had defended political prisoners too well and were now pondering their dedication to the legal profession from behind bars.

My 'defender' did not run any such risk. He was primarily interested in whether or not I could pay his considerable fee of 300 Deutschmark. He disappeared as soon as I said that I had the money.

I didn't see him again until the trial the following week. His defence consisted of some legal mumbo-jumbo, the relevance of which escaped me entirely, and he actually left before the judges had retired. Soon afterwards I received a note saying that 300 Deutschmark had been transferred from my account. I had the uncomfortable feeling that I had wasted good money.

But I am running ahead of myself. The trial took place on 4 April, 1944. The court was conveniently close to the prison and a guard took us there, locking us temporarily in a dingy court cell. Promptly at nine we entered the large court room. The accused were seated on the left with their lawyers in front. The judges occupied the ornate chairs behind a massive baize-covered table and the prosecutor had his own dais on the right.

When the gowned judges entered all present stood up and everyone, except us, raised the Hitler salute. All three looked distinguished and were decidedly old and fat. By contrast the prosecutor was young, thin and pale. Looking at his ashy, hollow-eyed face I wondered whether the death sentences he demanded and the executions he had to attend had finally got the better of him. The public gallery at the back seemed to be packed with people and I wondered why. Certainly, there was no one there we knew.

As soon as the judges were seated, the prosecutor stood up and asked for the public gallery to be closed. State security made that necessary, he added. Everyone left. They filed out one by one, each turning around at the door and raising the Hitler salute like marionettes in a puppet-show. If it had not been for my splitting headache and my high level of anxiety, the humour of it all would have made me smile.

The reading of the charges began, followed by questioning. I was astonished how superficial the questions were and how carelessly the documents had been perused. The charge was that we had listened to the BBC from the end of October 1943 until the middle of November. Actually we had listened to it every night since the radio had become operational. The letter of number two in our little group had been intercepted in September and our confessions on the basis of that letter implied that our *Deutschfeindlichkeit* — hostility to Germany — was of much longer duration. Yet no one put two and two together and we, of course, were the last to draw their attention to it. I had a growing suspicion that all the proceedings were irrelevant and the outcome a foregone conclusion. The judges looked bored, but had an obviously fascinating discussion amongst themselves during the speeches of the lawyers. It was clear that their conversation had nothing whatsoever to do with the matter in hand!

Then I did something unpardonable which haunted me for years afterwards. It was at the end of the proceedings. The presiding judge asked if we had anything to say before they retired to discuss the verdict. By this time my morale was shot. I have since read somewhere that prisoners who have lost one-third of normal bodyweight often become deprived of all ethical sense and that some have murdered their own relatives for a crust of bread. What I did was almost as bad. The nonchalant way my freedom was choked to death, the losing battle for dignity, the terror of the trial and the despair about physical survival had clearly snapped my dwindling integrity.

I stood up. I should have denounced the entire miserable charade: the fat judges, the fanatical prosecutor, the care-for-nothing lawyers, the inhumanity of Nazism, the louse-infected prison, the utter inadequacy of food, the corruption of guards, the immense cruelty of fellow prisoners.

Instead I apologized for my *Deutschfeindlichkeit*, asked for clemency and shifted the blame to the much older man in our group, who had owned the radio and in whose room we had listened to it. True, he had a criminal record in the Netherlands and his close friendship with the village whore of Kleinwanzleben had not exactly heightened the esteem in which he was held. Yet we had been one in our anti-Nazi sentiment. My little speech to the court was the most dastardly thing I had ever done. I had obviously reached a low point and after it was all over I felt like a rat turning on other rats when the going gets rough.

The judges interrupted their conversation to listen to my apology and outburst, but seemed unimpressed. I obviously had not even dented the dreary morning's exercise. My agony, servility and hypocrisy had not struck a chord. Instead, I had now completely destroyed whatever was left of my integrity.

The judges left the court to consider the verdict, which gave me a much needed opportunity to calm down and come to my senses. The entire trial began to appear as a hazy dream in which my acute headache and mental anguish were the only real elements. I was reminded of the trials during the French Revolution which I remembered from high school history lessons a few years previously. The prosecutor Fourquier Tinville had demanded and obtained the death sentence of people without giving the slightest attention to their cases or pleas. Were we similarly victimized?

The judges soon returned. Fouquier Tinville would have probably condemned us to death for listening, but fortunately the judges gave us only two-and-a-half, one-and-a-half and one-and-a-quarter years *Zuchthaus*, or prison with hard labour, with a simultaneous loss of civil rights for three years.

Back in the court cell I met my two co-conspirators for the last time as it happened: we were sent to different prisons or parts of prisons. They berated me for my little outburst, but seemed to write the event off quickly as of little consequence, or as the product of a mind warped by misery. They were more interested in discussing the pros and cons of a long prison term. If the war finished before our terms were up, we would be all right. However, if the war were to drag on we would run the grave risk of being sent to concentration camp and that would be the end.

We pooled our information about the difference between the normal prison and the *Zuchthaus*. To the Germans a *Zuchthaus* was much the worse sort of penal establishment.

Only long-term criminals were sent there. Yet we had also heard that it was geared to a longer stay of prisoners and that therefore, if anything, conditions would be slightly better. This proved to be correct.

For years after the trial I felt gnawing guilt about my grovelling perfidiousness in court. It was easy enough to explain it and even explain it away. But what was wrong with my inner strength if it could so readily slink away at the very time I needed it most? I was brought up to be anything but a weathervane or a chameleon. And this was exactly what I had become the first time a real crisis had presented itself. How could spinelessness be turned into backbone?

The answer came after much groping. I began slowly to comprehend a number of things. First, that the Christian view of forgiveness and pardon fitted hand-in-glove with my experiences. How could I possibly forgive myself when this fickle self was the actual centre of my universe? Not even the most sophisticated form of self-delusion could turn fickleness into strength. It was like lifting oneself up by one's bootstraps. Yet it became possible if the fickle self received its strength from another point of reference. If Christ is the mainstay and partner, not only can forgiveness be total, but his strength can and does flow into the believer, providing strength where there is weakness and faith where there is perfidy.

The other slowly dawning discovery was that the low point I had reached was in actual fact a prerequisite for firmer identity. Paul had said that one had to become incredibly empty in order to be filled with Christ and all of a sudden this acquired new meaning. The conviction of my own sins was the only avenue for salvation and wholeness. Integrity was not possible if one tried to rescue the few bits left over from a now defunct ego. It had to be given up entirely and had to be rebuilt from scratch with the aid of the Holy Spirit.

In the manuscript I wrote about my experiences in April 1945, I carefully avoided the painful episode of my little speech. And yet it was the beginning of a healing process for which I am now grateful. Liberal theologians and ministers can never fully understand the centrality of the conviction of sin and the free offer of salvation by a crucified Saviour. This is because in the intellectual world of humanism the basic securities of life have never been radically denied. The ground and growth of Christianity are vested in those who have descended deeply into the depth of despair — amongst the ugly, the despised, the sufferers, the down and outers, those who have reached rock-bottom. It was thanks to the incredible personal chaos into which Nazism threw me that the equally incredible serenity of the Christian faith could become mine. Not all the time, but at least some of the time, for it can never be possessed, but only gratefully accepted as undeserved grace.

11

Typhus

SOMETHING HAD GONE WRONG, I did not know what. An indefinable feeling of horror hung in the air. It seemed to spring from person to person and take hold just as a red-clawed beast clutches one's throat in a nightmare. Yet nothing was said. Only if one were sensitive could it be read on the faces of the guards and the trusties ladling out the thin soup, or distilled from intonations and the way people talked in the corridor.

It was the end of April. I had been put into solitary confinement with nothing to do and no-one to speak to. The *Zuchthaus* sentence had suddenly turned us into dangerous criminals to be kept separate from everybody until transport could be arranged. I had re-read the weekly library book twice. It was a second-rate book about the First World War, glorifying the exploits of a particular regiment. Boring to the extreme! I had also polished the linoleum floor until it gleamed, any further effort proving useless.

The major excitement of each day was picking vermin from my prison shirt and trousers. The lice played a game of hide-and-seek. They would come out of their favourite haunts, the seams, whenever they felt my warm flesh rubbing against the cotton. And as soon as I felt their tiny feet I would tear off my clothes and crush the lice between two nails. But the cold would make them retreat hastily into their dusty hideouts and I would make them feel safe again by putting my things on and repeating the process. Outwitting my 'torturers' was the prime diversion of the day. Actually worse than the lice were their tiny glistening eggs. They were almost invisible and hatched on my body which took strong and energetic exception to the insult. Yet the survival of the fittest had made this particular brand of louse indefatigable: they would attack and propagate remorselessly. Nevertheless I won the battle: by the time the mysterious sense of horror began to ooze through the cracks and crevices of Magdeburg prison, my cell 307 was virtually free of lice.

One day the sense of horror began to take shape. I had climbed on my stool in order to get a change of scenery from the four naked walls. Between the slanted, opaque slats of glass on the other side of the bars I could see a section of the inner courtyard near the prison hospital. This time I saw prisoners carrying a stretcher with what appeared to be a lifeless body. Then another and still another. What was going on?

Information of any kind was hard to come by, the most innocuous bit of knowledge being used as a little power ploy. Even the most elementary questions were rudely dismissed as potential boat-rockers. Questions seemed to be an affront to the guards. As obedience alone appeared to slake their thirst for recognition of power and authority, I had learnt to become a good listener. Snippets of conversation in the corridor and reading between lines of casual chit-chat had become my way of learning. Direct questions by contrast could very easily reveal ignorance and then the fragile relation of inequality between guard and prisoner could break down and reverse itself. It was more sensible to avoid the dilemma altogether! The prison system hated intellectuals and students. They were given the most menial and undesirable of jobs and I soon learnt to keep my university education a deep secret.

The next day the prison routine began to crumble. The airing of prisoners in the outer courtyard was suspended. Work crews stayed inside. And then I heard one guard complain to another that they, too, were locked in and had to cope with emergency accommodation in another wing. The entire prison had been put under quarantine and the prisoners on the stretcher had all died of typhus, roaring through the prison like a raging fire.

Gradually, I pieced the picture together. One prisoner after another had succumbed to horrible intestinal cramps, diarrhoea and high fever. Their starving bodies soon weakened to the point of no return and 127 men, twenty-five per cent of the population, died in a couple of weeks. The little prison hospital could not cope with the influx. Other buildings on the grounds were readied for the sick. But the turnover was high and many of them were bedded down on the mattresses still warm from a previous, unfortunate occupant.

After twelve of the well-fed guards died, emergency measures became strictly enforced. Yet not much could be done until the epidemic had run its course. Typhus was transmitted by lice and the reason fewer of those in solitary confinement caught the disease was that infestation had been easier to control. In the larger cells the lice often won out over the humans. I may very well owe my life to the judges who had so sternly sentenced me to *Zuchthaus*, thereby separating me from the rest of the prison population.

When the epidemic began to abate, the entire prison was evacuated. The firm of Krupp in Magdeburg had a big delicing centre. Trucks carried prisoners all day long to their bathhouse where large drums heated our clothes to 100 degrees Celsius. Meanwhile we were herded under scalding hot showers. Imagine our astonishment and horror when on return we were unloaded at the slaughterhouse instead of the prison.

Meat had become increasingly scarce in 1944 and large sections of the abattoir were now unused. Straw had been spread over the entire surface of two large lofts and this is where we spent the next few nights until the prison could be disinfected from top to bottom.

The attics proved to be perfect for keeping inmates. There

were no windows and only one exit. Escape was impossible. Yet there were compensations. Moving from assigned places was forbidden, but with ingenuity and luck one could exchange places with others and so friends often managed to be together. The food supply also greatly improved. There was more bread. The pea soup was thicker and everyone got more. Those in charge of the distribution could not now barter away the leftovers.

Guards were everywhere. They moved around somewhat, but one of them was permanently stationed in the area of those waiting for execution. There were not many on death row, but they drew quite a bit of attention. Their hands and feet were shackled and we felt very sorry for them. We could not get close or talk with them on account of the guards. By contrast, I was much closer than I cared to be to the four new cases of typhus which broke out in the loft. They seemed to suffer immensely and were soon taken away in order not to demoralise the rest of us.

Finally the prison was ready again, although the ground floor was still being disinfected when we returned. We arrived via the municipal health building where yet another delousing took place. It was to happen three more times in three different installations throughout the city. Even so, there were still lice around, as the prison committees in charge of inspecting our clothes discovered to their dismay. And so the order went out that all prisoners had to be shaved from head to foot. Not even the hair in our crotch region could be safe for lice any more.

Back in the cell I had to sleep on the floor in a sterilised blanket; the mattresses had not been disinfected as yet and would not return for some time. A Croat from the ground floor was also billeted in my cell and he proved to be rather inventive. There was no room for both of us on the floor and after thinking a while he found the perfect solution. He shoved the table over the toilet in the corner and spent the night curled up on top of it.

There were now very few new cases of typhus. Yet early

in June I contracted the disease, or at least I thought I did. On that particular day the guard had given me the job of mopping the corridor. This guard was the only sympathetic one I had ever met or would meet. He was an old man in his sixties and had been in prison work all his life. He had never been a Nazi and did not even pay lipservice to the Hitler worship around him. He was kind to all prisoners. The other guards treated him as the village idiot, but he was no fool; no prisoner could take advantage of him and there was no corruption or false dealing with food when he was around.

He was a pious Lutheran and usually went around the cell block with a well-used Bible. He would read it every day, but as he knew most of it by heart, I suspect that he was merely checking his memory. He expected the return of the Messiah any day and loved to talk about heaven. In great detail he would describe the golden apples, the delicious food and the Lord on his throne. Some prisoners thought he was a religious maniac.

He provided me with a Bible which I read dutifully every day. There was nothing else to do and it gave me a heart-warming glimpse of what life could be and had been for hundreds of generations before me. I became particularly fond of the Psalms. I remembered the austere cadences of the sung Bourgeois versions in the village church of Ophemert where I had grown up. It was as though a previous life had returned while I was reading. Yet that previous life also had an unexpected relevance for my predicament. King David had groped for the rock of salvation while wrenching his heart out because of imminent defeat. Wasn't that essentially my situation as well? I tried to compose psalms myself on toilet paper with a stump of pencil I had filched from somewhere.

Every day the guard came to visit me, ostensibly to inspect my cell, but actually to practise his little sermons on me. I had several debates with him which usually finished with him having the last word. Strangely enough, this was not because I felt compelled to pay homage to his authority – he was much more secure than any of the other guards – but because through listening I seemed to get the full benefit of the relaxation and edification I felt after his visits. I was enthralled to discover that there were Germans of his calibre around. He never discussed Nazism, politics or even the war. The gospel was to him the great news. I did not agree with his visions. Yet to me they became signs of something very precious: a soul at peace with himself, a solid trust in God's plan for the world, a mental calmness which I had not been able to muster.

It was this guard who one day in June had put me to work in the corridor. It had not been hard and yet it had thoroughly exhausted me. The reward had been an extra portion of soup at lunchtime. In the afternoon I became violently ill. My stomach chopped and churned as a tugboat in a hurricane. Then diarrhoea set it. By now I was convinced that typhus had caught up with me. I lay down on what I thought was my death bed. I did not even call the guard. It made much more sense, I feverishly thought, to die on my own rather than surrounded by others in hospital. Nothing could be done anyway: there was no cure for typhus. The big thing was to cope with this new crisis as well as I could. I had not been too brave in other crises: maybe this time I could summon more mental stamina. I read some of the Psalms describing God as the mainstay in times of trouble, a refuge in disaster, a stronghold against the enemy. I was in severe pain, yet I fell asleep, vaguely surrendering myself as King David had done, and feeling a peace accompanying the surrender.

When I finally woke up, I was much better. Obviously the unusual job in the morning and a stomach unaccustomed to being full had played havoc with my system. It was good to be alive and to know that my starving body still had some counter-punch left in its hidden recesses!

Part III
Halle Zuchthaus

12

Train journey

THE LONG-AWAITED DAY finally arrived. Early in the morning of 28 June we were told to get ready for the transfer to the *Zuchthaus* in Halle. The guard in charge of supply took our prison uniform and made us take a shower; then he handed us our civilian clothes in which we had been arrested. Ordinarily it would have been a treat to wear again well-fitting apparel. Not for me, however, nor for those who had also been guests of the Gestapo.

The holes in my socks were larger than the remaining mesh of wool and only on close inspection could one recognise socks in the rags. Even worse were the shoes. Each sole was worn through in the middle. The upper parts had been allowed to dry out in the prison store room and unfortunately had set in an altogether wrong shape. Only bulldog courage and much pulling and pushing had the desired effect of fitting them over my painfully cramped feet. Every step I took in them was agony. My grimy coat without buttons put the finishing touch of my transmogrification into a tramp.

We were not to leave until the noon meal which, wonder of wonders, consisted of sauerkraut and potatoes instead of watery soup. The farewell gesture was much appreciated, yet we were very pleased to leave Magdeburg. The industrial North with its Junkers aircraft factory had been bombed extensively and black clouds of smoke were still billowing from what had once been an oil refinery. Soon the entire inner city was to be destroyed.

On departure my Dutch friend and I were flung into the smallest of possible cells in a Black Maria. It was intended for one person only and the guard had to push and kick the door before it could be locked. Fortunately, the railway station was not too far away. The driver insisted on driving at break-neck speed, thereby both aggravating and shortening our ordeal, before the departure of the train to Leipzig.

In front of the station we joined another party of prisoners all manacled together. Someone had forgotten to bring an extra pair of handcuffs for us and after some mutual recriminations a policeman solved the problem by walking between us, holding onto a sleeve of our coat. We marched to the platform with armed policemen on both sides of the convoy.

We were obviously a sorry sight. The crowds milling around the station stopped in their tracks to gape at us. Some of the faces reflected disdain for the ne'er-do-well delinquents they imagined us to be. Despicable spongers on the State we were! And this at the very moment when the Fatherland was in grave danger and needed all the help it could get to win the war! I remember two older well-dressed ladies shaking their little grey heads and whispering to one another, fascinated by the sight of us. I am sure they were proud of the healthy looking police force marching resplendently next to us, protecting their fragile existence against vicious villains. They must have been pleased with our undernourished state. After all, it proved that evil was being punished and that rogues and robbers got their well-deserved wallop of suffering.

On the platform the train to Leipzig was already waiting. There was one carriage just for us. The small windows were heavily barred and the glass was opaque rather than transparent. Inside was a passageway with numerous little doors each leading to what can best be described as a narrow yet deep closet or cabinet. Four prisoners were prodded into each of these. We could not even move to take off our coats and soon it became stiflingly hot. The stench of sweating bodies was unbearable.

I had been the lucky first one to enter and this meant that I had been pushed against the little barred window. Close to eye level a small corner of glass had been broken off and as soon as the train began to move, a little draught of air started to circulate. It was hardly sufficient to provide adequate ventilation, but at least something to be grateful for.

Once outside Magdeburg I made an earth-shaking discovery... it had become summer. Peering through the little opening brought tears to my eyes. Here we were speeding through the countryside on a cloudless summer day. Fields of yellowing grain, green hills in the distance, a checkerboard of farms, orchards and vegetable gardens smacked me in the face. The beauty of it all was like a physical assault shaking me from my head to my cramped feet. Having been brought up on a farm the seasons had always been important to me, but I had taken them for granted. We were arrested in the winter and the dreariness of a city prison without signs of spring had enveloped me as a cloak. Everything within me and without had been winter. Now the coldness and cruelty of the Nazi world was destroyed in one fell swoop. Summer had overcome all that was base, ugly and corrupt.

I was transfixed by the scene only one of my eyes could see. I did not dare to turn my face around for fear my fellow prisoners would see my tears. Being from the city, they would not understand. They could not even imagine what nature meant to someone from a farm, nor could they possibly conceive that all of a sudden the earth had again become the source of immense power it had always been deep down in my psyche, that it had flooded my resilience with unrelenting force, filling it to the brim. It had been so utterly unexpected. First the humiliation of looking like, and being treated as, a good-for-nothing vagabond and then this glorious, achingly beautiful train journey.

It took all my inner resources not to cry out in ecstasy, not to celebrate the rebirth of a quenched spirit, not to shout out loud that summer had defeated Nazism and all that was corrupt and ugly within me. I felt cleansed and born again.

Nature in its full glory had trampled underfoot man's castles of self- glorification, the thousand year Reich, the incredible suffering inflicted on those who stood in the way of making the nation or the Party the supreme idol!

In Halle my cramped feet felt the earth again. The local police force was waiting for us on the platform exactly where the train came to a stop. Compared with Magdeburg there seemed to be twice as many policemen, as though the journey had made us twice as dangerous. Here, too, we were marched briskly out of the station, the police fully aware of the civic importance of the occasion and the onlookers swelling with virtuousness according to their perception of our decadence.

On the square, our column was swallowed up by the Black Marias taking us to our various destinations. Our vehicle came to a stop in front of what looked for all the world like a big country house on a broad boulevard lined with large oaks and shady chestnuts. Through a gate we came into a courtyard which in no way destroyed the idyll of bucolic languor; only cackling chickens were missing! We entered a room at the end with white-washed walls and clean wooden floors and here the illusion came to an abrupt end. The guard on duty made us jump to attention which is how we were to stand until the warden could see us. Apparently the big man was busy and meanwhile for at least a quarter-of-an-hour the guard watched for the slightest of our motions. Not even an involuntary twitching of a finger or the movement of an eyeball escaped his attention. He obviously loved the thunder of his own voice and the effect it had on novices who anxiously acceded to his wishes.

The warden proved to be somewhat friendlier than his assistant. No doubt the blasting in the outer office had been a regular routine to accentuate both his authority and his reasonableness. He gave us a fatherly speech, in all probability the one he had ready for young first offenders. Throughout our stay in Halle *Zuchthaus* the fact of being a neophyte in crime was stressed. *Gestrauchelt* — one who has stumbled

— was written in large letters on the little card displayed on the little cupboard in whichever cell we occupied. The card also showed the date of arrival and the last date of sentence, but never mentioned the kind of offence as had been the case in Magdeburg. This meant that here inmates could concoct any story they fancied about their pasts, whereas in Magdeburg their fantasies were constrained by the brutal fact of the black and white information on the cupboard. In Magdeburg everyone knew that I was a *Rundfunkverbrecher*, that I had committed an offence against the broadcasting laws. Here cell mates had to take my word for it.

Through the back door we entered the *Zuchthaus* proper. Row upon row of barred windows paraded along the six storeys of the long cell blocks. We entered the storeroom where we received a new set of clothes, all stamped 6/6/44. That was certainly a change from the prison where any old bit of clothing had to do. The trousers were black, but had bright yellow stripes on the sides and an equally bright red letter 'J' for *Justiz*, or justice, on one leg and a 'V' for *Verwat*, or department, on the other. Obviously escaping in pants of this kind was out of the question. The jacket was of a much quieter design: it had a yellow band only around each sleeve, although the letters 'JV' on the back were just as large. The outfit was completed by a little round cap which prisoners had to wear at all times unless they were addressed by a high official.

Freshly decked out in our new uniforms we were taken to a cell in one of the long blocks I had seen before. Like the warden's office it, too, was whitewashed with cleanly scrubbed wooden floor and table. Soon we received our evening meal. It also seemed an improvement: half a slice of bread and a half litre of rice. We had not seen rice for a long, long time and although our perpetual hunger did not diminish much in Halle, the quality of the food seemed to be better. Our survival chances seemed to have improved slightly.

In bed that night I recounted the happenings of the day. The climax by far had been the train journey. It had enthralled me to the point of giving me renewed confidence and hope. It had restored motivation .

Even now, forty years later, I recall the event vividly. I *had* a religious experience that day. It taught me never to underestimate the potential of nature or secular causes as pivots for re-orientation, Archimedean points for leverage. Again and again individuals in all cultures have received remarkable strength from a point of reference beyond themselves. It is as though they were grabbed by that point of reference and pointed in a different, more fruitful direction. It is as though mental union came into being miraculously at the very moment that an inward, self-centred search changed into a reaching out to a plausible, outward benchmark or point of order transcending the self.

Yet I also learnt in those intervening years that these experiences can fade quickly and become flashes which burn out without leaving much of a trace. Only some frames of reference have withstood the onslaught of the ages. In the West, Christianity has been intricately interwoven with tradition and culture allowing countless individuals in each generation to be revived and made whole in Christ, the source of salvation. More importantly, Christianity has dealt much more comprehensively with an exhaustive pattern of forces of alienation, breakdown, evil, fragmentation, tension, immorality and falsehood which are often summed up in the concept of sin, and the opposing forces of integrity, goodness, wholeness, peace, serenity, morality and truth which are often summed up in the concept of salvation.

Another frame of reference, the ancient healing memory of identification with the ecosystem that may have been coursing through our veins since the ancient hunting days of the race, seems somehow less relevant than many competing systems today. This may be the reason why, in later life, the world of nature and with it, social causes such as social justice, human rights, democracy, world government or the basic principles of my sociological profession such as objectivity, analytic competence, deep understanding, have tended to lose their central position in my system of meaning. They are too segmental. The wideness of their healing mercies has not been great enough. By contrast, Christ's mercy has proved to be all-encompassing. Yet relevance and rationalisation do not explain faith. Jesus' act of redemption on the cross and my acceptance of this act as a source of salvation stand above the mundane studs of relevance and rationalisation. Man is never explained exhaustively by his needs, nor is he realistically met by a figment of his own imagination or by the reasonableness of his thought. The rock of Christ is taller than man's thought and firmer than his most enduring fantasies.

13

Work

'YOU ARE VERY LUCKY,' the prison official in charge of employment said. It was the middle of July and he had just assigned me to the prison crew working in the Hallesche Maschinenfabrik und Eissengieserei, the Halle Machine Manufacturing and Iron Foundry.

After arrival in the *Zuchthaus* I had been put in solitary confinement. This was not to punish me or to separate me from less dangerous inmates, as had been the case in Magdeburg: there just was no room anywhere else. It also gave the guards a chance to keep precise track of my conduct. Was I sufficiently subservient? Was I polite to the guards? Did I keep the cell clean? Was I anxious and despondent and therefore escape-prone? Did I work well on my own?

I did not mind being in solitary provided I had something to read and something to do. I received my weekly library book — in contrast with Magdeburg the library took note of preferences — and every morning a large parcel with sheets of paper was brought in which I was to fold into envelopes. Many inmates were difficult to live with and in Magdeburg I had discovered some of the advantages of being by myself. The section guard was a blustering nincompoop, but I did little he could complain about and after a week he 'promoted' me to envelope gummer. This earned me an extra quarter litre of soup every day.

My 'promotion' came about through the enlistment of a youngish German prisoner who up till then had pasted the envelope borders. I had shared his cell for a day to learn the 'trade' and it had been a rather unusual experience. He definitely had a screw loose. Halfway through a conversation about nothing in particular he would climb on his stool and address an imagined audience. The speech was utter gibberish and yet had the right rhythms and solemn sounds. Then, just as suddenly, he returned to the table and gummed furiously as if to make up for lost time. At first I thought he was playing a joke, but he was deadly serious. The army had probably rejected him because of his mental state. But now it was desperately short of recruits and after all he was not in any way dangerous.

After another week as gummer I must have been recommended by the section guard for still 'higher' duties. The employment official summoned me to his office where the already mentioned observation about my good luck was made. As he did not elaborate I kindly asked him why he thought so.

'Well,' he said, 'the Hallesche Haschinenfabrik is very small, but of great significance for the war effort. It supplies our glorious armed forces with much-needed supplies.'

Usually German officials were too convinced of their own values to be aware of possible others, but he probably noted how unimpressed I was with this kind of good luck. Through his many contacts with foreigners, he might have even learnt to take the official rhetoric with a grain of salt. At any rate he added: 'You will get extra bread for breakfast and at lunchtime there will be a quarter litre of soup extra for heavy work.' This certainly was more impressive!

That same day I was transferred to the C-wing of the prison occupied by the prison crew to which I had been assigned. At 4.30 the next morning I had to stir from my bed. Then came breakfast and the roll call in the courtyard. We were arrayed in twenty rows of four prisoners and each had to call out his number in the line-up. This meant working out one's own place in advance in order not to interrupt the rapid-fire counting. The best way to draw attention to yourself was to hesitate during the counting. The guards with their loaded revolvers hurled expletives at anyone not fast enough to their way of thinking.

On that first morning I had no trouble with my number, but I stood out as a rose in a weedpatch through my new uniform. All the others wore drab and dirty clothes covered with oil and grease stains. Their thin bodies and yellow faces betrayed nothing of the luck which was supposed to have come my way. Worse was the foul smell of sweat and grime hanging around the entire group. Soon I would not notice this any more as I would be like them. Yet there was a five minute shower every Saturday after work and every two weeks our underclothes were changed. Neither were there any lice. Only the outer jackets and trousers looked like a dirty pair of overalls and actually functioned as such.

After the head count, the senior guard (Herr Oberwacht-meister — all hell broke lose if you forgot the 'Ober' when addressng him!) gave a curt command and off we marched through the forecourt with its vegetable plots for staff and through the gates to the boulevard lined with oaks.

The vigorous march lasted a quarter-of-an-hour and came to a halt in front of an empty tram. It had a sign on the outside saying that there was seating for twenty-four persons and standing for eight only, but every day eighty prisoners were pushed in with the guards doing their best to press them together. After all, they had to have some room for themselves at each of the entrances. Later that year ninety-seven prisoners were transported in the same little carriage. On that occasion the guards were flushed with annoyance, and fussed, foamed and brandished their pistols until every-one was inside. It took a lot of doing and we were told the phone line between the factory and the prison was very hot indeed on that day! The next day the numbers had decreased substantially!

The tram took us through the entire, beautiful, inner city. In contrast to Magdeburg, Halle was built on hills and was proud of its many tree-lined boulevards. The tram journey proved to be an ever-recurring pleasure. Not far from the factory we got out. Another column was formed, but it was soon split when one guard took his workers to *Werk 1*, on one side of the street, and the Oberwachtmeister took the rest with him to *Werk 2* on the other.

Everyone was now dispatched to their various working stations until just the guard and I were left. He took me to a large hall where there was so much clanging and banging that speech was impossible. Apparently this was the area where casings for tall cylindrical rockets were made. They were about three metres tall, had round heads with openings for what I supposed were detonation devices and had skirt-like bottoms which stood on the shop floor. These were called *Heizbehalters* or heat containers — I assume for rocket flames. The guard had his own little office at the back, but even with the door shut I could hardly hear. He finally got all the information about my age, sentence and employment experience on a sheet of paper and then showed me a forbidding looking document which warned that any spy or saboteur in the factory would be executed. I had to sign a form saying that I was aware of all this and that I did not intend to do any spying or sabotaging for a foreign power. I did so without much hesitation. The heavy security blocked any possible subversion attempt even if I had been so inclined! The Nazi Party and management actually seemed to prefer convicts as workers because they were so effectively segregated from the free world. Everybody was extremely security-conscious. It seemed that parts of the V weapons were manufactured here and this did explain the paranoia. Towards the end of the war, concern for security became almost obsessive. One political prisoner was executed when he welded only the outside of two cannon parts together, forgetting about the inside.

I was assigned to the only section of the factory which had not yet changed over to military production. It was still producing and replacing turbines and boilers for sugar and chemical factories.

My job was to help the welders when the containers on which they were working had to be turned around. I also assisted the foreman with measuring the pressures which the various boilers could endure. All this took place in a large foundry tall enough to even house vats thirty metres long and three metres in diameter.

The foremen were German, but the workers mainly Italian and French prisoners of war. The foremen particularly disliked the Italians. The latter operated from the principle that the least possible amount of labour should be expended and practised the principle with a devotion bordering on the religious! No work of any kind was carried out when the foremen were absent. The French at least appeared to be less shy of hard work. There were also a few free French, Poles and Russians around who worked for wages.

I became good friends with one of the free Frenchmen. He knew about our effort to keep the French prisoners of war informed about the news from the BBC and how this had led to our prison sentence. He felt that he owed it to them to help me. He mailed letters which I wrote surreptitiously while in the toilet cubicle to friends from my student days. They worked in Berlin and Leipzig, but some of the addresses had changed and only through one of these contacts did I receive money and food. Unfortunately, I was transferred very soon afterwards.

Contacts of this kind were ruthlessly destroyed if discovered. The guard had a master key for the toilet cubicles. He would sneak in ever so quietly and suddenly open the door. One of our fellow workers was caught writing a letter and was punished with four weeks of bread and water in solitary confinement. The guard would hide himself in the most unusual places. Suddenly he would emerge when you least expected him. He also had his spies amongst the civilian German workers. One of them warned both the Frenchman and me one day that he would report us if we kept seeing one another so often. Fortunately the Frenchman worked close by, but from then onwards we always conversed without looking at one another and often from some distance. All Germans hated us talking in French or English which they could not understand. The guard even made it a rule that only German was to be spoken, which of course we did when he was around. Never did we talk about politics or news from the front in German. It was just too dangerous.

Least reliable were the criminal prisoners. We were all equally hungry, but one could at least trust those who were sentenced for a political offence not to report anti-Nazi statements to the guard. In this respect I felt even freer than in the so-called 'free' world. But those who had committed a criminal offence were quite happy to pass on any gossip to the guard for a crust of bread. It was often difficult to hide from cell mates and fellow workers extra food one had been able to get hold of or letters one had received. I am sure that the employment official did not have this in mind at all, but the good luck of working outside consisted primarily in being able to establish connections with the free world.

The radio in the canteen was another unanticipated lucky perquisite of working at the Halle machine factory. Part of the canteen was assigned to us, but we could always listen in to the radio in the section partitioned off for the free workers. And so we kept well abreast of the news from the front. Later in 1944, however, the radio simply disappeared. It was surely not an accident that this happened at the exact time that the Allied invasion in France became a triumph. But then my French informant, who was quite excited about the progress, more than made up for the absence of official news. By drawing maps in various dusty spots with the latest Allied advance prominently marked, he kept me very up-to-date. All this went on without anyone knowing, because I erased the maps as soon as I had seen them. The problem with all this drawing in the dust was that we soon ran out of dusty spots to draw in. I wonder whether anyone ever caught on to the reason why there was so little dust in the area where we worked!

At six o'clock in the evening work stopped. The guard

would put a bit of cleansing powder in our cupped hands. It was poor stuff. Only after much scrubbing could we remove most of the grime from our hands, necks and faces. Some civilians had soap powder which did a much better job, but only occasionally could we get hold of some of it. Then we would march to the tram again, tired yet pleased that work had opened opportunities (psychological as well as material) which the employment officer certainly did not have in mind when he told me how lucky I was to become part of the Hallesche Maschinen prison crew!

14

Suicide

LATE ONE EVENING the corridor was abruptly woken by
a scream of agony. It was followed by urgent pounding on a
cell door. Then it was quiet again. Obviously the inmate was
waiting for a guard to appear. When nothing stirred the
pounding was repeated, this time with even greater fury.
The gaoler was long in coming. Only a skeleton staff was on
duty at night and one guard was supposed to look after an
entire block. All he could do was to make the rounds at
regular intervals.

Protocol for emergencies required the gaoler to first find
a colleague. Sometimes a cry for help was a ruse. Once,
apparently, a guard had quickly responded to what he
thought was a crisis and had been promptly knocked uncon-
scious on opening the door. One prisoner had put his uniform
on and left him gagged and bound on one of the bunks. All
three had escaped with the keys, but had been caught when
they tried to scale the six-metre wall. Although it had happened long before our arrival, prisoners loved to go over the
story with a fine toothcomb, adding, I suspect, many apocry-
phal embellishments. Yet they always finished with how they
would have improved on the plans and how they would have
carried if off more successfully. As it happened, they never
had a chance.

On this particular night it took both guards at least five
minutes to appear. They turned the lights on and opened the
door. Inside they found two of the prisoners badly shaken.

The third was hanging from a hook on the top window choked by his suspenders. He was cut loose but had already died.

Next morning the grapevine provided the details. The inmate had been a middle-aged German who had murdered his quarrelsome, nagging wife. He had seemed a rather gentle person, somewhat of a loner. He usually went his own quiet way and did not seem at all passionate. Yet he had stabbed his wife with a carving knife when she had belittled his manhood once too often. She had been a prim and proper middle-class housewife, but he was happy to remain a blue-collar worker in a bicycle shop. Once he had confided to a cell mate that she had taunted him sexually, refusing his overtures one minute and blaming him for lacklustre performance the next. He had received a very long sentence and his family had abandoned him completely. He had made no friends in prison, had nothing to live for and so had decided to end it all.

It was all rather tragic, but it was by no means the first suicide. Every night the prison officials insisted on removing all cutlery and the pail of water from each cell. Suicide, they felt, set a bad example. Some might catch the disease and upset the morale which was precarious enough as it was. Prisoners might blame the oppressive prison system for the event and become even more restive and mutinous than they were imagined to be. And of course there were always a few of the more soft-hearted guards who might wonder whether their own tyranny had something to do with it all!

Outside the walls, members of prison crews had much better opportunities to kill themselves. Everyone had access to all sorts of tools. Once a thirty-year-old Czech opened the veins in his wrists with a file in the toilet of the machine factory in Halle. I was on the same crew, but did not know him very well. He was shunned by some of the other foreign prisoners, partly because he was rumoured to be pro-Nazi and partly because his offence was criminal.

He was found by the guard who regularly patrolled the

toilets because it was here that anything illegal was trans-acted. On this occasion the guard saw blood trickling from under the cubicle. He opened the door with the master key he alone possessed, but it was too late. The guard himself had been rather chicken-hearted on this occasion and had invei-gled another prisoner to clean up the gory mess in exchange for an extra portion of soup at lunchtime.

On the way back to prison that night the crew was buzzing with the news. For the first and last time the Czech was the centre of attention. Who was he? What had he done? Why did he kill himself? The misery of being a foreigner in a country which despised Czechs, the malnutrition, the terror of incar-ceration, the rejection of his country of birth, no relieving hopes and beliefs, no compensating fantasies or friendships — all seemed parts of the picture as it was gradually recon-structed by the gossip. In our little group the conversation about him took an interesting turn: would we have done the same if we had been so obviously desperate? No was the answer; escaping was a more sensible outlet for desperados. Then you had at least a ten per cent chance of making it. Even death through execution — the remaining ninety per cent — was preferable to taking your own life.

A young Frenchman stood next to me in the tram on the way back. He had been studying for the priesthood, but had been caught for some anti-Nazi offence before he had been able to finish. He whispered to me that under no circum-stance would he commit suicide. It was not just that the Catholic Church forbade it. No, he honestly felt that life was a gift from God and that he had put him here for a specific purpose. Who was he to usurp the power that God alone pos-sessed? He had suffered as much as all of us. Perhaps even more because many prisoners had ridiculed his intended profession. If there was a God, so the argument of the despisers went, why then did he not rescue him from the ordeal? To them he had answered that God might very well have a hidden purpose in mind. Regarding suicide, he added, the present suffering was as nothing when later in life or in the afterlife it all would make sense and God would reveal himself. Suicide would destroy the very nurturing process of which he was part.

There were other ways to make life in the prison system tolerable. The fantasy world of books was one. The prison library in Halle was well provided with well-known English and American novels, all translated into German. The major Jewish authors, such as Thomas and Heinrich Mann, Stephen Zweig and Wassermann, had all been removed, but I remember reading many books by Upton Sinclair, the Canadian author Mazo de la Roche, A.J. Cronin, Pearl Buck and particularly the Norwegian author Knut Hamsun whose Nordic romanticism and pro-Nazi sentiments had made him into somewhat of a cult figure in Germany. All his books were there, as were other Scandinavian authors such as Ibsen, Hansen, Bjornson and Gulbransen.

There was little time for reading, unfortunately. In Magdeburg the library had been much worse, but there the opportunity to read was greater. Books had made up for much of the pre-trial uncertainties. In Halle, however, after an eleven-hour working day we would be so tired that we fell asleep before a page was turned. Only on Sunday was there more chance to relax with a book for any length of time.

Work itself was another important way of keeping the wolf of despair from the door. It was usually both dirty and boring, but there was enough variety and pressure to leave little time for morbidity and desperation. It might not have been fulfilling, but it was certainly better than idleness and being left alone with one's gnawing hunger and twisted thoughts. It took the attention away from self and turned the mind to the tasks at hand.

Most prisoners also got a kick out of beating the system. While at Magdeburg I had been put to work for a few weeks on the Hubbe crew. The Hubbe factory produced margarine and prisoners were used for loading and unloading wagons with rape and other seed. Some of it was edible and, whenever the guard had disappeared for a few minutes, we would eat and chew a mouthful of the stuff. Old hands warned us against hallucinations from too much of it, but we were never long enough on the job to suffer the consequences.

I derived more satisfaction from stealing carrots in Mr Hubbe's garden after the guard had turned his back. The owner of the factory had a big house in the country with a large vegetable patch. A group of eight of us had been taken there to spread manure, till the soil and clean debris. However, in the middle of the garden was an earth- and straw-covered cache of carrots. While the guard was having his cup of tea in the kitchen, seven of us shielded number eight by working between him and the kitchen window. Hiding behind the heap, he dug right through the soil and the straw to where the carrots were. All of us happily shared the loot and for once we were not hungry that night.

Events like these lightened the day and some really cunning prisoners played the game of beating the system to perfection. Most of us, however, were less clever. To us, working and talking with others was an important antidote to the kind of despair leading to suicide. All prisoners were part of the nationwide war effort. Their labour had become more vital than their punishment. But work meant cooperation with others and so communities of like-minded people emerged. Loneliness was suspended in the act of working together. Most individuals received strength, not from deep debates, but from casual conversations while doing one's job.

Not long after my arrival at the machine factory I was assigned to a German fitter and turner who had to construct a big cooling drum. There were large plates on both ends, with numerous round holes through which long three centimetre pipes had to be threaded in such a way that they would come out in the corresponding hole on the other side. This meant much discussion back and forth and it was fun getting it finally right. My boss was tall, blond and rather taciturn. He had three young children and had been exempted from war service because of his job. He had obviously been instructed to keep his distance from convicts, but yet he was very considerate. He was a hard worker himself, but slowed down when he noticed how I wearied quickly through underweight.

Most members of the prison crew had been there for a year or more. They had had a chance to develop enduring relations with civilian co-workers. They relished the jobs in which they had become experts. More importantly, they had come to an understanding with some of these co-workers who would leave left-over crusts wrapped in yesterday's paper in pre-arranged garbage cans. By their work they had built up a sense of self-worth, enhanced further through casual banter. They were least likely to kill themselves.

So were the political prisoners. The war was going well and hopes of an early defeat of Nazism were strengthened whenever one of us managed to get hold of a more or less recent newspaper. Political prisoners usually had sufficient personal stamina to stand up to collective pressure. Stubborn individuals with a strong ego to defend and with solid hopes of being vindicated were unlikely to commit suicide.

15

Operation

I LAY ON THE OPERATING TABLE of the prison hospital. The pain was excruciating.. There was no doctor, let alone a surgeon, but the guard had a diploma in first aid. All his life he had harboured ambitions of being a surgeon, but for some reason or other — I am afraid it had something to do with his intelligence — they had never been realised. And now was his chance. The instrumentarium of the hospital was non-existent. The guard, however, was the old-fashioned type anyway and he still shaved with the kind of razor you have to sharpen on a strap before use.

Fortunately, he had read about the importance of sterilisation and so he brought water to the boil on a hotplate in the little kitchen. It took a while; long enough, at any rate, for him to remember that if he was going to act the piece, he owed it to his fellow surgeons to be attired in the appropriate manner. It might be regrettable that there were no surgical tools, but at least he could do justice to the paraphernalia of office. And so he produced a surgical gown from somewhere, put it on and began to sharpen his razor on the strap. Then he dipped it in the water which was boiling by now and was ready for the job in hand.

But I have to retrace my steps in order to explain how I came to be on that table. In August 1944 I was given the task of cleaning the large, ten metre boilers of the heating system of the Halle Machine factory. They were half filled with ashes and it was my job to crawl into them — they were less than a metre in diameter — and on return take as much of the stuff with me as I could. It was quite uncomfortable. The ash was very light, whirled up at the slightest touch and penetrated whatever I wore. And so I would sneak up on the elusive enemy, take a deep breath, put as much material as I could in a bucket, retreat, throw the bucket in a container and run for fresh air. Once the dust had settled I would have another crack at the fiendish phantom.

For once the guard was sympathetic. On the first day he decided to check on my progress by peering into the pipe. I was backing out in a cloud of ash and he beat a hasty retreat. From a safe distance he saw the cloud dissipate and me appearing from it as a ghoulish apparition with actual arms and legs. It was the middle of summer. The ash mixed very well with perspiration and settled as a mudpack on all exposed skin. And so for the first time the guard actually told me to take it easy. Normally he had everyone run on the double, but now he told me to leave work half-an-hour early to shower and clean up. As shower-taking was a weekly rather than a daily privilege, he must have been really impressed.

I did not see much of the guard after that. He had instructed the boilerman to watch the entrance in case I had sinister intentions and so I was cared for, he thought. Little did he know that an empty boiler pipe is an ideal place for whatever cannot bear the light of day. With a hand-held lamp deep inside the innards of the tube I read not only the newspaper provided by my French friend but anything else available. Actually on the pretext of the ash having to settle down I worked less than two hours per day, lazing around for the rest of the time, curled up comfortably against the side.

After weeks of this I had become ill. Ash had penetrated the footsores which had not healed because of malnutrition. Blisters had formed on those parts of my feet where the prison slippers had bruised the skin during the 'airing' in the first weeks of my stay in Halle. Socks had not been issued on arrival — everything was getting scarce — but the guards had continued to insist on a fast pace during the half-hour march in the courtyard. They had overlooked the effect slippers had on bare skin. It was too late by the time we were allowed to 'fast walk' without anything on our feet. Bandaids and ointment were available, but all of us were too undernourished for new skin to form. In my case ash had penetrated the footsores and the tiny lice wounds left from Magdeburg days.

I have never discovered whether my illness was actually connected with the poisonous gases in the boiler tubes, as my fellow prisoners said it was. Later that year three prisoners were rumoured to have died because of these gases. The kind of coal available for heating at this stage of the war was apparently rather inferior. Whatever the cause, I became desperately ill. Also my knee was badly infected. In a matter of days it doubled in size. A red stripe ran all the way up my thigh and it looked as though blood-poisoning had set in.

Again the guard was unusually kind and let me stay inside, an unusual move from this guard who assumed that everyone was a malingerer unless proved otherwise. One of my Norwegian friends had been forced to go to work one day with a high fever. I wonder whether I got so much consideration because my ghostly appearance a few weeks before had scared him out of his wits. In no time swelling and fever became so bad that I could not climb out of the bunk, let alone put on trousers over my grotesquely deformed leg.

And so I was transferred to the prison hospital. It was situated in a newly built wing above the place of execution and next to the book-binding section. I was only half-conscious when I arrived, but I still remember another, younger guard suggesting to my 'surgeon' that I seemed to be a case for the downtown hospital; however, he was overruled and so the operation took place.

It was actually very simple. The guard with the first aid diploma pushed a flattish bowl under the offending knee. There was, of course, no chloroform or other anaesthetic agent, but as I was half-conscious this did not seem to matter.

While the guard who had been overruled held my leg straight above the bowl, his older colleague carefully selected the right spot for the jabs he then deftly administered with his razor. Actually I am probably a bit unfair ridiculing my 'surgeon'. He seemed to know what he was doing. He did not cut major arteries or muscles. A mass of blood and puss flowed into the bowl. By now I had passed out altogether because I do not remember him putting a drainage tube in the wound and bandaging it up.

When I came to, I found myself in a ward with nothing but seven beds and barred windows. All the other six beds were occupied with dying inmates or those who had broken a limb. We were looked after by another prisoner who, I soon discovered, had the best job of all twelve hundred prisoners at Halle. He would get full rations for whoever was alive in the ward, but as the dying were also beyond eating, he had their portions as well. He was one of the very few who never went hungry.

For several days he could eat my food, too. I slept almost continually. Even during the periods of greater lucidity I had no appetite. My knee was still twice the normal size, and the guard decided again to put his razor to use. This time he hit the jackpot; the swelling decreased dramatically and, after a few days, my appetite also returned to normal. Unfortunately for the supervising trusty, I got better at the wrong time. The dying had died and all prisoners on the ward were recovering. I remember him complaining that this had been his leanest period on record. Still, the rations were relatively sufficient for individuals who had to stay in bed all day, and so I slowly recovered.

After two weeks I began to walk again — first, very slowly and hesitantly, but soon I could sally forth with a walking stick. I remember reading a lot in this period. Books about Australia and New Zealand had particularly tickled my fancy and I kept dreaming about them as ideal places to be. So much sunshine. So much freedom. So much opportunity. And above all, so far away from what had become crystallised in my mind as a good imitation of hell — Nazism, war-torn Europe and the acute nearness of death on the ward as well as below us, where every Tuesday and Friday dozens of individuals were executed. But more about this later.

One of the ward rituals was weighing. It appealed to the structured bookkeeper minds of the guards. We sometimes wondered whether the figures and the neatness of the record were not more important than keeping us alive. Certainly dying had become an exercise in bookkeeping. The tragedy of it was subsumed under the various recording motions necessitated by the event. After all, the figures had to always balance. Slipping away was the ultimate horror. Registration was the remedy for dread.

I still weighed fifty-five-and-a-half kilograms when the first session was held after the operation. Although my normal weight was eighty, I still had not lost the dreaded one-third body weight. Two others on the ward weighed only fifty-one kilograms and were much closer to the danger point. Yet they, too, were on the mend and were looking forward to rejoining their prison crews. Barred windows depressed them deeply. By contrast, work outside the prison walls made them forget the terror of confinement.

Every two weeks a downtown doctor visited the hospital. Halle was obviously short of medical personnel, but it was the prison rule that some kind of health inspection was to take place at regular intervals. When it was my turn, I asked him to have a look at my lungs as well as my knee which by then was doing fine. I suffered from chest pains and occasionally coughed blood. He checked me and then told the guard to send me to the hospital downtown for an X-ray; however, the order was never carried out. Instead, I received a little bottle of Baldrian for whatever the guard was convinced ailed me.

During my recovery — I could now walk with a stick — I was summoned to the warden's office. The warden had a visitor who was introduced to me as the Swedish consul. Then I was offered a chair which was highly unusual. A prisoner never sat in the presence of a guard and particularly not in the presence of a higher official. So I began to realise that the visitor was an important person whom the warden wanted to leave with the impression that prisoners were well treated.

Apparently my indomitable mother — I was her eldest — had written to high and low about the danger I was in. Her fertile mind had in no way slowed by the lack of response. If anything it had spurred her on to greater zeal. And so she had conceived the idea of getting the Swedish Embassy involved. Sweden was one of the very few European countries not at war and took a lively interest in the fate of prisoners and the Red Cross. The Swedish ambassador in turn had instructed the consul in Halle to inquire about my health and to see whether my plight could be eased in any way. And here he was with my mother's letter.

How was my health? By now I had been trained to always comply and never complain. Moaners and whiners were vilified. Yet the chair and the courteous treatment had given me visions of better days and had fortified my courage. And so I told the consul about my work, my illness and my underweight. I saw the warden frown while jotting things down. When I was finished he said that, of course, the operation had weakened me and that generally 'boys of my age' had huge appetites, but that he would see what he could do. Nothing happened, naturally, and I was actually lucky to be exempted from the treatment meted out to grumblers: I had seen guards and their henchmen being devilishly unfair to defenceless prisoners whose reasonable complaints had displeased them.

Then the consul brought up the matter of study books. Quite accidentally I had mentioned in the half-yearly letter I had been allowed to write home that I missed my music and books for my economics courses at Amsterdam University. Actually, I had not missed them that much, as there was little time left after a sixty-hour week. But here it was brought up officially and there was certainly plenty of opportunity now in the hospital. The warden was agreeable and so the next week I received Max Weber's *Economy and Society* and a book on economics by Sombart.

There was a condition attached to being allowed to study: once back in the cell blocks I would have to do it on my own or, in other words, I would have to consent to solitary confinement. This was more of a burden to the guards than to me. To keep a prison crew together, prisoners had to be moved frequently and I became an additional problem in logistics. I mentioned the single-cell requirement only on those occasions when prospective cell mates were out-and-out crooks. Both the guards and I forgot about the rule when I was billeted with the Norwegians with whom I had made a solid pact of friendship.

The problem of solitary study, however, did not crop up while I was in hospital. I was glad when the day arrived for me to start work again. We were now in September and I had been away from the prison quarters of the Hellesche Maschinenfabrik crew for more than five weeks. When I returned my friends hailed me as someone who had returned from the dead. And so I had!

16

The Norwegians

I OWE MY LIFE to two Norwegians and one German, all three serving long sentences for high treason. They rescued me from the brink where death and underweight meet. After surgery and recovery, I returned to the boiler shop where heavy work used up more calories than the prison food provided. Our metabolism was by then finely honed to extract maximum value from caloric intake, but it just was not enough.

It became worse later in 1944 when rations were further reduced. One day four of us carried a fellow prisoner back to his cell. We never saw him again. There were others who likewise yielded up the ghost, but I particularly remember the one I helped carry. The long nose in the pale face with the sunken eyes are even now deeply engraved on my memory. His eyes had the same doleful, heart-rending quality of those of a favourite horse dying in a stable with all of us around.

More than likely I could have been that man. However, before going into the story of my redemption, I have to return to my first encounter with a remarkable body of nine Norwegians, all political prisoners and all caught red-handed for subversive activities. I met the first one of this group a few weeks after my arrival. He only spoke Norwegian and a bit of broken German. All he had was primary school education. He was a bow-legged sailor who had been caught in a boat ferrying escapees to England. He had a wife and three young children somewhere along the rugged coast of Norway and I discovered later that he had lost track of them and they of him.

In the cell with him was a highly sophisticated German with two doctorates. His career had been meteoric. From prison official he had risen to warden, then to judge of a court in Dessau. His knowledge of prison corruption was vast and with open-mouthed wonder I watched him smuggling messages back and forth to his beautiful wife still living in the large villa which he showed us a picture of. At first I did not believe the story of his meteoric career, but later I met inmates to whom he had given harsh sentences and who lampooned him in no uncertain terms. He was an active member of the Nazi party and his very agile mind had been put into its service. At least so it appeared. We had some very interesting discussions about objectivity and truth. Correctly, as it turned out, he saw these qualities as dependent on, or certainly interdependent with, social circumstances and culture. But at the time I vehemently defended their independent status.

He had fallen as fast as he had risen. He was sentenced, he said, because he had taken his money out of Germany and invested it in a Swiss bank. Of course he failed to mention, as I learnt later, that this money had been milked from an orphan fund he administered!

At any rate he was a fount of knowledge. He knew how the prison system worked. His promotion through the ranks had been the result of his capacity to minimise costs by cutting expenses of food and labour and to maximise profit by negotiating lucrative contracts for prison labour with industry. He had also been present, he said, at a very hush-hush demonstration of the latest V 8 weapon which destroyed all life in a circle of sixty-four square kilometres. Although by now the Allies had successfully invaded France, he was entirely convinced of Germany's victory once Hitler decided to use this ultimate weapon.

When I joined the sailor and the judge they had just squabbled about bread. The general rule was that in each cell, prisoners took turns in having first choice of whatever had to be distributed. Usually there was not much difference, but sometimes one piece was slightly larger. The judge had ignored this rule and had put himself in charge of distribution. Invariably he kept the better piece for himself. The sailor had given him a withering look, but had kept his cool. The story repeated itself that same night, but the next morning I happened to be closest to the trusty handing out the bread and I let the sailor have first choice, which, of course, earned me a withering look from the judge!

This small, rather insignificant, event was another item leading to profound disillusionment with intellectuality per se. My schooling and upbringing had trained me to believe that man's reason was the glorious capping-stone of creation. But here was an example of a very intelligent person with a sharp, logical mind who had somehow failed as a moral being. He was good-looking, authoritative, the kind who automatically attracted people's attention when entering any gathering. He was a clear, quick thinker, a genius in debates and yet he would cheat this sailor with his broken German out of his due, a slightly larger crust of bread.

The judge was not an original Nazi. In all likelihood he had joined when membership had become advantageous. But then the Party had taken over and, like a leech, had sucked his native intelligence for its own twisted purpose. His intellect had become a whore dancing to the tune of whoever paid the price. Yet, I began to suspect, wasn't this usually the case? Wasn't intelligence on its own a monster or a marvel according to the basic commitments it served? But if this were the case, which commitment could make it a marvel and which a monster?

The sailor by contrast did not sparkle at all. He was incomparably worse off and yet he never lost a sort of instinctive steadfastness and dignity. He was polite and yet natural as though he owed all other beings, even Nazis, at least token respect. He was clean and reliable. He was not moody, but

affected the morale of the cell by a ready smile and the whis-
tling of a Norwegian tune if he felt like it.

The judge was always talking about himself, his accom-
plishments, his predicaments, as though he was desperate
for someone to allay his anxieties by admiration. What he got
instead — at least from me — were questions about his basic
beliefs, about the problems of running a prison, about the
ambiguities of judging, about the comfort of Party membership. He was always sorry for himself, basically because the
world, even the Nazi world, had not let him get away with
his self-aggrandisement and self-enrichment. I felt drawn to
the Norwegian, not necessarily because I was in tune with
him politically, but because somehow he seemed to be the
wisest of us all.

I was not long in this particular cell before I met the other
eight Norwegians for whom I developed similar respect. We
were all working on the same prison crew. They proved to
be always responsible, honest and incorruptible. Their cells
and clothes were usually slightly cleaner. Yet the guards
hated them and they were likely to get the heaviest and dirti-
est work. All nine had been in the prison with hard labour in
Hamburg when that city had been smashed to smithereens
by allied bombs and when the days had been as dark as the
nights. They were the survivors of a much larger group, but
many had died of tuberculosis. For an entire year they had
not seen meat or sausage — here in Halle we still received
an ounce per week — and they explained that starvation in
Hamburg had been much worse than in Halle, something I
found hard to imagine.

Their integrity was unbelievable. Not even death could
shake their political convictions. Their hate for anything
German was fierce. They derived all moral strength from
this hatred. I used to wonder about the simplicity of this
black-and-white thinking. But it certainly was a most effective morale booster. Their moral strength seemed to be more
robust than that of the best of my countrymen. It was certainly tougher than my own! Fortunately for me they had

formed a very high opinion of anything Dutch. They had been locked up with Dutch resistance workers in Hamburg and I vaguely understood that some of the Dutch backbone and intransigence had infected them. Seeing that I was the only Dutchman on the crew, I was soon adopted as one of them. Obviously I was the undeserving recipient of goodwill established by fellow countrymen, most of whom had perished in the Hamburg holocaust. The sample of Dutchmen there must have been rather unique and yet they came to represent to the Norwegians what Holland was all about. It was also the other way round. The type of Norwegian they represented was, I am sure, a-typical. Yet even now I continue to think of Norwegians as exceptionally courageous and imperturbably balanced.

Most of them were sailors caught ferrying escapees to England, but there was also a university student, an office clerk, a fisherman and a truck driver. Almost all of them were tall and blonde. They were popular in the factory because of their friendliness and capacity for hard work. Even German foremen liked them, although they certainly never got their full trust. Neither was their kindness unlimited. As a matter of fact it was often only a thin veneer covering cool aversion. They always read one another's letters and supported one another through thick and thin. I am sure that this had made the sailor as durable and rooted as he was compared with the brilliant judge. Later in the year I met the group of them almost daily during the air-raid warnings, when all prisoners had to assemble in the factory washroom.

At one fairly long stretch of time I was billeted in a large corner cell known as the Norwegian block. It was highly unusual for countrymen, particularly if their offense had been political, to be put together. But towards the end of 1944 when the effective separation of prisoners during air-raids became impossible, the rule was relaxed. Yet the Norwegians had received permission to be together long before that, through the unyielding efforts of a Lutheran pastor from Norway who had come to visit them twice a year and had lobbied very hard with the prison authorities to obtain the privilege. I assume that he had used the argument that prisoners with high morale were in the long run the safest. Little did the prison authorities know that the high morale was forged primarily by keeping anti-German sentiments alive!

After two weeks with the boilermakers I again weakened visibly. At the time one of the Norwegians, Eilif Vikre, who was a student in economics at the university of Bergen, came to me and mentioned that there was an opening in the X-ray section where he worked. He had talked about it with the other prisoners there, an office clerk from Bergen, Zygmunt Zachariassen, and Carl Wienecke, a German teacher who was serving a twelve-year term for high treason — he had been an official of the Social Democratic Party. They all told me that their German boss would recommend me to the guard and to management for the job.

I needed no time to think it over. This was my redemption! The work required brains and no brawn. It meant precision work: the right voltage and amperage for the exact time, precise positioning of the photographic plates on the inside of the container, accurate labelling of plates and developing them in the correct chemicals for the prescribed six minutes.

The work was dangerous. A heavy leaden door and partition shielded the apparatus and us from the flame container to be X-rayed. No-one could survive more than three minutes of direct exposure and therefore a bright red light was turned on over the main entrance through which the containers were wheeled in and out. When the light was on, our cabin was also out of bounds to the guard and so we could use that period for undisturbed reading and writing.

One of the guards thoroughly disliked this restraint on his spying. He had a genius for sneaking up on anyone and could be watching you for some time without you knowing. But the cabin was out of bounds. He could have stayed there during the photographing if he had so desired but then, of course, he would not be able to catch us. Once he risked his life by rushing through the red light, but we heard the main door slam shut and when he entered the cabin we were innocently watching our dials, the newspaper safely hidden under the desk. This was also the only guard who ever needed us. He just was no good at paperwork and at the end of each month he would somewhat sheepishly seek our help with the books and accounts he had to keep about working hours and work performed by prisoners.

It was fortunate that the boss supervising the X-ray operation was the only staff member in the factory who actually favoured political prisoners. He and his secretary would leave so-called scraps left over from lunch in the garbage can of their office. He defended the exclusive use of political prisoners in his section by exaggerating the danger of the job. And then he would add that we alone had sufficient education to understand the nature of X-rays.

I owe my life to those fellow prisoners who got me a soft job at the very time that the health of all prisoners was deteriorating seriously and rations were being cut back even further. Even having to write this is difficult. Admitting not only that I desperately needed physical, but also mental and moral help, is saying that I do not measure up to independent, rational manhood. Western civilisation has made rational individualism an ideal by which we judge ourselves. Actually it is a false ideal. To need redemption is to be more human than to deny it.

To realise this was an important step towards becoming a Christian. Jesus can never be the Saviour of anyone who has not first overcome the barrier of self-sufficiency, whether imagined or real. And as self-sufficiency is least precarious amongst those who are successful (such as the judge who was hopelessly entangled in his own self-glorification), Jesus' statement that it is more difficult for a rich man to enter the kingdom of heaven than for a camel to pass through the eye of a needle is profoundly true.

The moguls of academia, where individual rationalism is

the essential assumption, find it almost impossible to be saved by Jesus because the emotionality and the dependence of the affirmation goes right against the grain of the foundation of their success. And yet their commitment to this principle is not any less irrational, and often their 'saving' remains unanalysed and is much narrower than the Christian one.

My experience with the judge and the Norwegians, indeed all death-defying incidents and unspeakable suffering, were ever so many avenues to increasingly deeper understanding of Christian salvation. God's mercy to me lies incongruously not so much in the fact that he allowed me to survive it all, but more importantly in the way he prevented me from taking the easy way out and from making idols of the self, the nation, a congenial principle or anything else that humans can concoct and fabricate. And when all these crutches were revealed for what they were, the vision of Christ and his saving power had become all the more splendid.

The weaker the idols, the stronger the vision. It was only then that I received an answer to the question I put earlier: Which commitment can make intelligence and reason a marvel and which a monster? It was the Christian commitment alone which could do the trick of turning a potential monster into an actual marvel!

17

Bomb Disposal

IT SEEMED TO ME THE MIDDLE OF THE NIGHT when the light was turned on and the guard who was so good at spying and who hated our X-ray unit shook my bunk.

'Get up!' he commanded.

I felt like asking why this was necessary. After all, it was only 4.00 a.m. and Sunday morning, the only day of the week we did not work. However, by now I had learnt that guards hated explanations even more than they hated prisoners and so I just did what I was told.

Outside the cell my two Norwegian fellow workers on the X-ray unit were already waiting. In front of the cell block we joined a motley crowd of bedraggled men like us in dirty prison uniform. Yet the bright yellow stripes and equally prominent red letters 'JV' were visible even in the faint light of the courtyard lamps. As usual we had to array ouselves in rows of four and call out our number in the line-up.

Yet something was alarmingly different this morning. Instead of the usual two guards with loaded revolvers we were now surrounded by as many as twenty of them, all equally grim-looking and all heavily armed. They marched us to the familiar stop where we boarded the waiting tram. Then there was another ominous turn of events. The tram took quite a different route and carried us way outside the city. It came to a stop at what seemed to be nowhere. A melancholy November drizzle fell from a leaden sky and in the distance we saw the ruins of the city of Merseburg.

Merseburg was the centre of the German synthetic oil and rubber industry. It had been heavily bombed by the Allies the night before and our tram had come to a stop in front of some craters. We had to walk the rest of the way and soon were splattered with thin mud from soil thrown up by the explosions and softened by the rain. It stuck to our flimsy clothes and chilled us to the bone. Yet our brisk march kept the blood flowing.

The further we went the greater the damage seemed to be. There was not a single restorable house in sight. Pale and confused people were searching the ruins for lost relations and items of property. They were not frantic as one would expect them to be, but aimlessly resigned, as though an eerie phantom held sway over all their actions and thoughts. They scrounged as though they were dream-walking, holding up a damaged photograph, stroking a broken utensil or smoothing bits of torn curtain. They seemed to collect the shards and fragments of a past existence as though careful touching and reverend contemplation would somehow restore that past.

We came to a halt in front of what had once been the police headquarters. There were hundreds of soldiers and prisoners of war milling around. All had shovels and axes to clear the roads and gradually the square emptied. Yet we were left standing in a corner, obviously waiting until the authorities could deal with us. Finally it was our turn. Around the corner came a line of trucks with red crosses on their sides. Each was fully equipped with stretchers, first-aid kits, a first-aid attendant and a fireman. Each got its complement of twelve prisoners and five heavily armed guards. The fireman gathered us around and began to instruct us in how to tackle unexploded bombs. We had become a bomb disposal unit!

It took us some time to get over the shock. Yet the fireman, the first-aid attendant and the guards talked about the task at hand in a matter-of-fact way and their equanimity began to rub off. To them we seemed to be nothing but learners. If we were properly instructed, they appeared to assume, dismantling a bomb was no different from hanging out the washing or digging a hole in one's garden. And, of course, we had no choice. The guards had not asked for volunteers for the simple reason that there would not have been any. We were just conscripted. There was no redress. Foreigners who had subverted the German machine were lucky to be alive anyway! On top of that, the guard had selected the three of us from the X-ray section because our work was relatively light and the other members of our prison crew deserved their Sunday rest more than we did, he had reasoned.

Off we went, packed in our Red Cross truck. However, streets were blocked everywhere and the driver had to back in and out so often that it was late morning before we arrived at our destination. And then to our scarcely concealed joy we found that the bomb had already been detonated and we had to go all the way to the other side of town to a new location. Here there were three unexploded bombs, one each for a crew of four. Ours had fallen behind a bakery in a heap of rubble left from a previous air attack. We moved the bricks, stacked the wood and began to dig. The bomb had come to rest six feet below the surface and we made sure it took quite some time to deepen and widen the hole.

In the meantime, the guards, the fireman and the first-aid attendant had found a sheltered spot out of the rain just far enough away to be out of range in case the bomb went off, and yet not far enough to lose sight of their charges. Occasionally the fireman would walk over to see how we were progressing and to give additional instruction. However, the deeper the hole became, the less visible we were and the more slowly we worked.

Then the air-raid siren went off. Near panic broke out. Memories of the previous night were still fresh. In no time we were hustled up and marched to the nearest shelter. However, the British prisoners of war who had been cleaning the streets had been ahead of us and the shelter was full to overflowing. This upset our guards no end. But the civilians around were even more panic-stricken. A woman with a child in her arms began to cry hysterically. Someone explained that the woman's mother was still buried under the rubble and the mood of the crowd began to be uglier by the minute. Then the mob began to demand the Britishers be thrown out because it was their air force which had caused the ruination. However, the guards of the prisoners of war held the crowd back with their bayonets. I suspect that they were less worried about the Geneva Convention than about their personal vulnerability if they had to leave the safety of the shelter together with their charges.

Fortunately, the alarm proved to be false. No planes appeared and we went back to our digging. Slowly and carefully our five hundred kilogram bomb was exposed. We did not dare use spades and shovels at that stage and scooped the soil away with our hands. Finally the bomb was completely unearthed, but then the fireman was busy with another crew and it was dark before we could remove the catch. We counted ourselves fortunate that our entire Sunday's work had been confined to the one bomb. Other crews had been less lucky and one of them never made it back to prison. Their bomb exploded on touch.

It was late when we saw the empty tram looming out of the dark after the long march back. We were miserable in our wet clothes and my Norwegian friends and I huddled together in a corner of the vehicle. Yet our spirits were high. We had cheated death again and we felt exhilarated by the crushing damage done by the Allies to the synthetic oil industry. The extra bowl of soup that day had not stilled our perpetual hunger and yet we were full of expectation. The lunch of the fireman had been wrapped in a very recent newspaper. We had retrieved it and, although we had only been able to read the headlines (we had tucked it away under our clothes for detailed reading at some later date), the news had buoyed our hopes for speedy liberation. Everywhere the allies were tightening the noose around the Reich.

Death and liberation. These were the two poles around which our entire existence revolved. Starvation, desolation and extinction were the supreme realities. And yet our young lives refused to be snuffed out. The Allied victory was around the corner. If the armies would only hurry up before it was too late! It was all a race against time, but the future was clearly with us and gave us a fierce strength. It was determinate and circumscribed, not hazy and obscure. It had outline and form. Justice would win out. Nazism would be eradicated and its roots would be relegated to everlasting hell!

There was a religious fervour about the future and my Norwegian co-workers were possessed by it. It determined morale and shaped the present. It simplified and uniquely focussed emotions. All the suffering was not in vain. It would be vindicated in the latter day. My friends were bonded together by common hate and common expectation. The future was not only glorious; it was theirs as well! And when this future would arrive all torment would be justified. They were as eager as Paul the apostle when he wrote that the entire creation was on tiptoe, anxiously waiting for the sons of God to come into their own and to rescue men from the tyranny of change and decay. Their hope was no less certain and gave meaning to all they thought and did; however in their case the tyranny was Nazism rather than change and decay.

Ever since, I have innately understood millenarian dreams. There is something electrifying, simplifying and inherently true about the second coming. The Lord is coming! The future delineates the present! Order will destroy man-made chaos. Meaning will spit in the face of meaninglessness! Salvation will conquer sin as surely as the resurrection follows the crucifixion! The sufferers will be washed clean in the blood of the Lamb and God shall wipe away all tears (Revelation 7:17). Deep down it all makes sense.

Delineation of time and morals has been man's traditional (and effective!) way to deal with uncertainty and change. I have no trouble understanding Jerry Falwell and the Moral Majority. Nor do I have trouble understanding why those who feel secure can afford the luxury of flexible thought and arrogant doubt.

In at least one respect, however, millenarian visions are different and actually more realistic than others. The hopes of most political prisoners were immediate, not cosmic. Their saviour was an avenging angel rather than a loving Christ. Their expectations were conditioned by man's victories rather than by God's action. And so after the war short-sighted hopes had to be re-adjusted. D-day did not usher in utopia. Neither war nor peace solved much of anything. If they thought about it at all, they discovered that man had to wait for a different sort of salvation from the one brought by armies of liberation, social legislation, the United Nations and psychotherapy.

Already while I was musing with my friends, I remembered some of these thoughts going through my head. But the thoughts were too young and intimate to put in words at the time. Surviving seemed to be all that mattered, and central to survival was the Allied victory. But if my now maturing view of people and situations had any merit, so I thought, the actual future — if there were any place in it for me — was not going to be so radically different. The only difference would be whether I believed that the future was in God's hands rather than in man's. I tended to look increasingly towards the former, if only because it made so much more sense in the long term. It also seemed to me that survival of the human race was now increasingly a matter of man's disorder being checked by God's order. And as far as I was concerned, if God was in that future then my survival was relatively immaterial and his coming again would surely be of much greater significance than man's puny battles, defeats, victories and physical existence. And this is what I still believe. God and Christ express the blueprint of order. In them wholeness is summed up. When they reveal themselves more concretely in events and persons, the future will be radically different from what it is now.

18

Onions for Christmas

CHRISTMAS 1944 WAS THE BLEAKEST I have ever had. Coarse wheat and rye bread was the main staple of our diet. Until Christmas our total ration for the day had still amounted to about three hundred grams, but after Christmas it was reduced to two hundred. The number of fellow prisoners who succumbed and were unable to march to work increased. Yet staying inside was worse, since the rations were lower and the prison had run out of fuel for heating. Even during the minus eighteen degree Celsius temperatures of that winter, the radiators remained as glacial as the mood of our guards. Those working in the X-ray cabin were fortunate. Electric radiators were necessary for drying the films and the heat was sufficient for the entire cabin.

We had become friends with a number of enterprising free Russians working next door. One night, just before Christmas, they sneaked out of their compound and went on a poaching expedition into the country. They did not find much, but they came across a storage shed with sugarbeets. Back in their barracks they roasted them and we very willingly shared the loot. Initially the Russians had not been generous, but then the unappetising bluish appearance of the pulp and its less than tantalising taste made them increasingly charitable with the leftovers and we made sure that nothing was thrown out.

However much everything else seemed to decrease, executions were on the increase, if the prison grapevine was at all reliable. I had developed some interest in decapitation since my stay in hospital which was above the place of execution. The more perversely inclined of my fellow sufferers had insisted on a careful count of the times the heavy axe of the guillotine came thundering down on the condemned. The entire building would shake and after an interval of between five to seven minutes (presumably to remove head and corpse) there would be another fall of the sharp blade cutting clean through the soft flesh and bone of the neck.

The German prisoners called the occasion *Schlachtefest* — butchering party — and we all knew beforehand when it was to take place. Every day, recovering prisoners were aired on the little courtyard below, but on 'butchering' days, usually Tuesdays and Fridays, we were kept inside. On those days the cells looking out on the tiny space were temporarily occupied by those to be executed and the guards apparently felt that our delicate recovery would not benefit from close observation of the condemned in their final hour. They were probably right.

One morning the executions did not seem to stop. They went on and on for almost three hours. The aforementioned inmates with the excessive interest in the macabre proclaimed the day a day of records: twenty-nine deaths. Of course they could only count the guillotine executions. There were also twelve gallows in the same hall, but they were relatively noiseless, as the condemned were gagged and the benches on which they stood disappeared rather quietly into the platform at the touch of a button.

One day I met a member of the prison crew who had worked for a while in the prison smithy. It had been his job once to unscrew the heavy guillotine blade from the frame, to sharpen it and mount it again. He had chanced on a rather talkative guard who had shown him how everything worked.

The hall was solemnly decorated in red, the gallows on a platform on the left of the entrance and the guillotine at the end. A condemned prisoner knew that the time was near when he was undressed to the waist and his neck shaved.

When it was his turn he was fetched by the two executioners who were dressed in scarlet (I saw them once in their outfit from the window of the hospital). They gagged him in order, I assume, to spare the delicate sensitivity of the officials who were to witness the proceedings. Then he was guided into the hall where the court official read the sentence, after which the executioners put his neck on the block. It was over in a few seconds and immediately room was made for the next wretch.

In the meantime, the head which had fallen in a basket partly filled with sawdust to absorb the blood was put with the body in a black, roughly constructed coffin. From the toilet window we could see the hearse taking it out through the prison gates.

Also on the increase round about Christmas time were the hordes of refugees fleeing ahead of the Allied armies. In the fall they all appeared to come from the region of Achen. After Christmas, we saw wagon after wagon from Poland and Pomerania crawling at snail's pace along the tree-lined boulevards of Halle. There must have been hundreds of thousands judging by the small sample we could watch during our short tram journey early in the morning and at night. The miserable parades showed us how suffering was not limited to the inside of our prison. The horses seemed too small and emaciated for the loaded carts. Thin-faced, hollow-eyed women and children sat under a carpet cover erected on top of all the belongings. The men and boys shuffled on either side. They seemed to have given up whipping their animals on to greater speed, as though there was nowhere in particular to go. They appeared as bone-tired as their animals.

Yet the Germans in the factory seemed oblivious to it all. They could wax amazingly indignant about the shortages and the bomb attacks, but the suffering of either prisoners or refugees left them cold. They shrugged their shoulders about the executions we mentioned, as though all this dying on the front or in their own backyard was just too much to absorb. They seemed to repress whatever was beyond the very narrow horizon of local living, as though they needed a hedge to protect their uncertain existence from even more bewilderment.

Christmas Day 1944 reflected all the misery of our environment. The cell was intolerably cold and it was our luck that the guard on duty was possessed by a streak of sadism far exceeding the one carefully nurtured by his colleagues. He began by implementing the rule that no-one was to be in bed during the day and that no blankets were to be used to keep warm. Not that two thin cotton blankets did much good, but at least they diminished the shivering. I tried to read but the cold interfered too much with my concentration. So I gave that up and started to pace up and down the cell, but this got on the nerves of my cell mates.

Further along the corridor, three inmates decided to flout the rule and had crawled into bed no matter what. The guard, ever-watchful, kept peering through the spyglass in the doors and when he discovered the threesome in bed gave them such a tongue-lashing that it certainly diminished our desire to follow their example. But after another frigid half-hour, we devised a somewhat perilous scheme, whereby each took turns keeping watch with one ear cocked to the door while the others kept warm under the blankets. It worked in that at least we were warned when the guard's footsteps came in our direction. Yet having to jump in and out of bed proved to be almost as unpleasant as enduring the cold.

The problem was that the guard suffered almost as much from the below zero temperature as we did and had decided to keep warm by patrolling the corridor more vigorously and frequently. He kept his spirit alert by chasing witless prisoners out of bed. To detect offenders was to him as exciting as catching a fish after much effort. It suspended all boredom and provided a splendid opportunity for testing lung power and vocal chords. We joined the game by not letting him catch us. It would have all been quite amusing, if only the temperature had been a bit more cooperative.

Yet Christmas Day was not all bleak and cold. There was

first of all the surprise gift from management: two onions. They came at breakfast. Neither before 1944 nor after the war would the gesture have impressed us in the least. Yet I doubt whether I have ever appreciated any Christmas gift as much as these miserable onions. I cherished them and kept them as long as I could, peeling off a little at a time and putting tiny pieces on the dry slice of bread. I can still remember their delightful pungent smell and their tangy taste. Our present affluence is doing us a distinct disservice by obscuring the value of little things. Overeating and the glut of possessions have created their own set of physical and spiritual problems, but being blase is never the concern of those whose central occupation is survival. And so all of us were very grateful for our two onions.

Without being overly nostalgic for something as dreadful as starvation and imprisonment and without being fooled by the windings and turnings of a selective memory, I find that the simple presents and the little conquests of those days are precious to me, even now! Simplicity has its own deep attractions in times when a self-imposed discipline alone can prevent us from becoming slaves of our stomachs and worshippers of our possessions. I guess that only with this in mind can one give a bemused and bounded affirmation to the question whether we should be grateful to the Nazis for providing generously and free of charge what in later life proved to be costly!

The Christmas service was another break in the bleakness of Christmas 1944. The Lutheran minister took an active part in prison life. When I arrived he had asked me — as he did all other prisoners — to write a short autobiography. He then discussed this individually with each of us. My interview with him did not go too well, maybe because I had been looking forward to it. I had done a lot of thinking and groping about religious questions both in the Gestapo camp and the Magdeburg prison. I longed to have the Christian part of me, for whatever it was worth, strengthened. I felt the Gospels and Paul's letters were uncannily relevant to my search.

Instinctively, I felt that if I could sort out some of the religious questions, I could cope more effectively with the torrent of change which had washed over me and made me lose my bearings. I had begun to suspect that there were hidden depths in Christianity which I had much too prematurely dismissed as drivel in my teenage years. And so I had hoped that the prison chaplain would help me along somewhat in straightening out what appeared to me a jumbled intellectual and emotional mess.

Nothing of the kind happened. At the interview we talked a bit about organ music and he let me play the organ in the church hall on the second floor of the administration building. Yet, however much I liked Bach, I had never been very good at playing him. In the village where I had grown up I had only managed to play for services after much practising for each separate occasion. And so my usefulness to him on this score was rather limited.

At the end of the autobiography I had written something about the emotionality of being saved by Jesus and I tried to pick his brain on this. He had looked at me with some surprise as though I was some kind of freak and said that surely musty piety of this kind was outdated at a time when the glorious Reich was involved in a titanic effort to advance civilisation. He was obviously more interested in the anti-Nazi feeling lurking behind my offense against the broadcasting laws. If I was ripe for conversion, he seemed to imply, Jesus was much less relevant than the German Reich. Loyalty to Christ and to the German war effort were one and the same thing with the latter having immediate and practical priority.

I left it at that and let him get on with his other interviews for the day. Later I heard other prisoners mention that the chaplain was nothing but a listening post for the Gestapo and that he was more dangerous for political prisoners than all the guards put together. Yet I continued attending the Sunday services which always began and finished with the Hitler salute. They were lavishly sprinkled with references to the Führer, God's protection of the nation, heroic soldiers dying unselfishly for a free Germany, and the messianic responsibility of the Reich.

Services were suspended when coal for the furnace ran out. Yet there was a Christmas service in the unheated hall. It was the same warmed-up Nazi broth. More than half the prisoners were foreigners and yet the chaplain insisted throughout on nailing his Nazi colours to the mast. All we seemed to hear was the bubbly foam of national sentiment and the farce of a Nazified Christianity.

Where was the universality of the Christian Church? Strangely enough, it was there in the readings about the suffering servant from Isaiah and about the birth of Christ from Luke. It seemed to whisper to me that the suffering Messiah born as a defenseless infant in a hostile society was at one with other marginals such as us. Over against the sermon, the readings seemed to preach that salvation was not with the establishment (Nazi or otherwise), but with the poor of heart who had put their burden on him. This was the unexpected consolation in an otherwise inconsolable, self-destroying world!

19

Freedom

ON THE FIRST DAY OF SPRING 1945 the gates of Halle *Zuchthaus* were unlocked and for the first time in fifteen months I walked through them unaccompanied by armed guards. The sun was out and the trees were beginning to bud. Like the trees, I had been restored to new life after the dreary death of winter.

Until the last minute I had been in fear and trembling that the Gestapo would transport me to a concentration camp and certain extinction. A guard had actually told me that no foreigners were released after expiration of their sentences: all were handed over to the Gestapo. And yet here I was.

The winter of 1945 had been gruesome. Prisoners had begun to die in their cells from cold and malnutrition. The great Russian offensive had swollen the columns of refugees and diminished the resources for civilians. In the prison, sentences had begun to mean less and less. Those with long ones had begun to think of themselves as fortunate; those with shorter ones were frightened by the prospect of transferral to concentration camp. The more we heard about the latter, the more they began to appear in our thinking as ever so many vortices sucking the unpalatable into obliteration, or as gaping, blood-dribbling mouths, munching on the undesirables and digesting them with fire in their cast-iron stomachs.

The stories about release had been very confusing. The Gestapo seemed to be playing a cat-and-mouse game with its victims, now pouncing, nor releasing, as though it was bored with the charade. The German communists, the social democrats and the Czech criminals were all transported to concentration camp as far as we could gather. Even a few of those who had committed minor criminal offenses were sent to Buchenwalde or Sachsenhausen, as though the party had decided that scum of any kind had to be skimmed off the Aryan genetic crew.

But then suddenly a long-term political prisoner was allowed to go home. In January one of my Norwegian friends finished his four-year sentence for sabotage and returned to Bergen. His family had promptly arranged for his escape to Sweden where he was now recuperating. And apparently all other Norwegians were released as soon as their time was up.

For several months I had been fervently hoping that the war would be over in March. All fronts were collapsing. By now our lines of communication with the free workers were well established and we received fairly recent newspapers almost every day. In the radiation chamber was a large wall placard with instructions for the use of X-rays. It looked for all the world as though it was firmly attached, but on the reverse side we had glued a map of Europe with the pins indicating the towns mentioned in the Armed Forces bulletins. The highlight of each day was moving the pins closer to the heart of Germany. Yet March had come and the Allies were still quite a distance from Halle.

The further I walked away from *Zuchthaus*, the less I trusted my luck. I had been given a letter from the warden to the police headquarters in Halle and I was now slowly convincing myself that on arrival I would be arrested again. I did not trust that letter and, with every step I took, I was more certain that it contained a directive for transportation to Buchenwalde. And so I thought of good reasons to avoid the place. I began by making a long detour via the farmer's market where only carrots were available without a ration book. I stuffed myself with them until my stomach began to ache.

It was now afternoon and I was still afraid of getting even close to the police headquarters, so I went to see the Swedish consul to thank him for his mediation and deliver a letter from a fellow Dutchman whom I had met the day before. It was with him that I had spoken Dutch for the first time in nine months. He had been in the underground, had served his sentence, but had not been released. As he had an advanced degree in chemistry he asked the consul to contact the synthetic oil industry so that it could claim him as an essential worker. The consul also promised to help another Dutch chemical analyst who had tuberculosis and was wasting away in the prison hospital.

From there I went to see a lung specialist who was recommended by the Swedish official. Since I was still coughing blood occasionally, I underwent a thorough test. The X-rays showed a variety of scars and the specialist signed a document saying that my undernourished state was likely to make things worse very speedily. He said, 'Wave both the negatives and the letter in front of any official responsible for providing you with ration books and travel documents.' This I did whenever I could.

It was now late afternoon and I finally gathered all my courage and delivered the letter to police headquarters. In retrospect I am still astounded at my own naivety. Why hadn't I opened that letter somehow? If it had said something about further transportation to concentration camp, I could have been well on my way in the opposite direction before they would have begun to smell a rat. And if it was innocuous, I could have spared myself much unnecessary agony. At the time I was probably still so convinced of the omnipotence and omniscience of the Gestapo that I dared not even think about something as illegal as opening official mail.

Fortunately the letter was harmless. It asked the police to check my passport and to provide me with a travel permit to Kleinwanzleben where I had been arrested; however, by this time it had become too late for train connections and so my guardian angel, the Swedish consul, booked me in what proved to be a first-class hotel. Yet food was scarce and I remember sitting that night in the restaurant waiting to be served by waiters who studiously avoided me. My grimy clothes, remnants of the Gestapo camp, had obviously made me into an unwelcome guest. And so I ended that night washing carrots in the hotel room basin and eating them until the stomach cramps reappeared.

There certainly was no welcoming committee at Kleinwanzleben the next day! No one expected me and all co-workers had given us up for dead. Almost all my belongings had been stolen and the boss in the administration under whom I had worked wanted to have as little as possible to do with me. To the Germans I was a phantom from the past indelicately haunting them. At least some of them must have felt guilty about cooperating with the Gestapo in my arrest.

Strangely enough, they all knew about the court case, the *Zuchthaus* and the *Ehrverlust*, or three-year loss of civil rights. They called a meeting of the union and asked their leader to warn management in case it had intentions to re-employ me. Making them work with a *Zuchthaus* felon and particularly one with *Ehrverlust* would definitely bring a hornet's nest about their ears, they said!

I was both amused and insulted at the same time. Yet no insult has ever been more useful! The union representation together with the letter from the lung specialist put a fire under the director and he moved heaven and earth to provide a travel permit for the Netherlands. This was normally hard to get, but it was there next day!

No time was wasted. Recuperation was only likely at home and the fronts were collapsing, soon making any train journey improbable! I scrambled as much food together as I could and put it in the old suitcase, one of the few remaining possessions not stolen, and set off. The bag of mainly carrots and turnips rattled around whenever I moved the case. There had not been much else to fill it with.

Travelling light, however, proved to have a unique advantage! Wherever I went the Allied bombers had been, too.

The trains could only move on the unaffected bits of track in the country. In Hanover one had to climb over and around the ruins of the downtown region in order to catch a train on the other side. Thanks to my lack of possessions, I could take all these obstacles in my stride and ever since I have luxuriated in easy travel by refusing to take anything more than a briefcase on any journey, including world trips. By the time I arrived near the Dutch border, the food was finished and the suitcase almost empty. I felt like throwing it away altogether in order to celebrate freedom even more, but then I thought that I might be fortunate enough to scrounge up some food to partly fill it again.

In Bentheim I caught what proved to be the last train before the end of the war to Oldenzaal in the Netherlands. When I arrived it was the 30th March and Good Friday. With tears in my eyes I drank in the vision of clean Dutch streets and freshly washed windows. I would be safe again. The ordeal was over. I had been at the heart of hell where Christ had descended on that first Good Friday. I had seen the depth of misery as Christ had experienced the ultimate horror on the cross. But now it was over. I had come home. I had drained the cup of misery to its dregs. It had been desperately bitter, yet Good Friday had proved not to be the end. I had also died to myself. The old Hans Mol with his arrogant belief in the divinity of reason was gone. He had become chastened by the scourge of war, rejection, cruelty and pain. He had stared death in the face, but incongruously death had sent him back on at least three occasions. He had been set on a path of trust and faith from where there was no return.

In Oldenzaal, the Dutch border officials were not just satisfied with papers being in order. They also had a swimming pool with disinfectant ready in which all returnees were asked to gambol in the nude. They obviously did not want German lice and infectious diseases in Holland. Further, because of my emaciated state, I was held under observation in case I harboured other communicable diseases. But none were found and the authorities helped me in finding lost relatives.

A cousin of my mother worked at the post office in Oldenzaal, but I had never met him and only knew his name. I found him and his family in a little house which seemed to be bursting at its seams. Like my parents, he and his wife were born in the province of Zeeland, the southwestern islands of the Netherlands. However, almost everyone from there had been evacuated because of the war and flooding. And so his mother — a sister of my grandmother — and other relations fled to Oldenzaal. I was taken in as well and, in spite of the scarce rations, they fed me as well as they could.

The next day was Easter Day. There had been rumours of the Allies breaking through, but it was all hearsay. And then suddenly, very early on what the Dutch call *Tweede Paasdag* or Second Easter Day, a holiday on the Monday after Easter, I woke up to excited shouts in the street below. Half-asleep, I walked to the attic window to see what the noise was all about. And there I saw Canadian tanks and soldiers coming through the narrow street and taking the town without any German resistance. Dutch flags, which had been forbidden for five years, were flying everywhere, and the inhabitants of Oldenzaal all of a sudden seemed to go crazy. All their pent-up fear and oppression disappeared. They were liberated, and so was I. We were all free now. All pain and hurt was behind us. We could start living again!

Easter and liberation. They belong together. I had almost died bodily. Yet here I was, yelling my weak lungs out at the sight of all those Canadian tanks and soldiers.

Epilogue

AFTER RECUPERATION, HANS MOL resumed his study in economics at the University of Amsterdam, but his heart was not in it. In 1946 he accepted a position as assistant to his uncle who was in charge of the administration of the Dinteloord Suikerfabrieken in Stampersgat, the Netherlands. In 1948 he carried out his prison dream of settling in the Southern Hemisphere. On the first Dutch emigrant ship to Australia, the *Volendam*, the Protestant/Reformed passengers appointed him their representative and on arrival he began a newsletter for them. The immigrants soon decided not to start their own Dutch Reformed Church, but to join the Presbyterian Church of Australia. Hans Mol himself was invited by this church to work amongst the Dutch on its behalf while also studying for the ministry. He was ordained in 1952 and appointed chaplain to Dutch immigrants in the main immigrant centres of Bathurst, New South Wales and Bonegilla, Victoria. By now the Dutch were arriving in their tens of thousands and in 1954 the church sent him to the Netherlands to recruit Dutch ministers for the Australian Presbyterian Church. This he did together with his Australian-born wife, to whom he was married in 1953.

At the end of his theological studies he received the prize for the best student in theology and as a result he was offered a scholarship at Union Theological Seminary in New York. Here he finished a Bachelor of Divinity degree in 1954 and a Master of Arts in Christian Ethics in 1955. His M.A. thesis was on the sociological astuteness of Karl Barth's doctrine of man and was supervised by Reinhold Niebuhr and Robert McAfee Brown. By now sociology had become his major interest and in 1960 he obtained a Ph.D. in sociology from Columbia University in New York on a thesis dealing with Theology and Americanisation. The thesis was supervised by Robert K. Merton and Sigmund Diamond. During his graduate studies he was minister of Bethel Presbyterian Church in White Hall, Maryland.

After obtaining a Ph.D. he was invited to a lectureship in sociology in Canterbury University in Christchurch, New Zealand. He moved there with his family, now augmented with three children, in 1961. In 1963 he was appointed fellow in sociology at the Institute of Advanced Studies of the Australian National University in Canberra where he wrote and edited five books: *Race and Religion in New Zealand*, 1966; *The Breaking of Traditions*, 1968; *Christianity in Chains*, 1969; *Religion in Australia*, 1971; and *Western Religion*, 1972.

In 1970 he, his wife and his four children moved to Hamilton, Ontario in Canada, where McMaster University had offered him a professorship in the sociology of religion. He is still there. At McMaster he wrote and edited eight more books: *Identity and the Sacred*, 1976; *Identity and Religion*, 1978; *Wholeness and Breakdown*, 1978; *The Fixed and the Fickle (Religion and Identity in New Zealand)*, 1982; *The Firm and the Formless (Religion and Identity in Aboriginal Australia)*, 1982; *Meaning and Place*, 1983; *Faith and Fragility (Religion and Identity in Canada)*, 1985; and *The Faith of Australians*, 1985.

He has remained active in both the Presbyterian Church and in professional sociological associations. From 1963 to 1969 he ran the Sociological Association of Australia and New Zealand as secretary-treasurer. From 1970 to 1974 he was first secretary and from 1974 to 1978 president of the Sociology of Religion Research Committee of the International Sociological Association. In 1985 he was the keynote speaker, opening the fifteenth International Congress of the International Association for the History of Religions at the

University of Sydney. He was visiting professor at that university for the 1985/86 academic year.

Other books by the author

Churches and Immigrants (1961)
Race and Religion in New Zealand (1966)
The Breaking of Traditions (1968)
Christianity in Chains (1969)
Religion in Australia (1971)
Western Religion (editor, 1972)
Identity and the Sacred (1976)
Religion and Identity (editor, 1978)
Wholeness and Breakdown (1978)
The Fixed and the Fickle (1982)
The Firm and the Formless (1982)
Meaning and Place (1983)
The Faith of Australians (1985)
Faith and Fragility (1985)